MANHUNTS

— denial of humanity

MANHUNTS

A Philosophical History

Grégoire Chamayou
Translated by Steven Rendall

PRINCETON UNIVERSITY PRESS

PRINCETON AND OXFORD

Originally published in France as *Les chasses à l'homme: Histoire et philosophie du pouvoir cynégétique* © La Fabrique-Éditions, Paris, 2010

Published by Princeton University Press, 41 William Street, Princeton, New Jersey 08540
In the United Kingdom: Princeton University Press, 6 Oxford Street, Woodstock, Oxfordshire OX20 1TW

press.princeton.edu

Library of Congress Cataloging-in-Publication Data

Chamayou, Grégoire.
[Chasses à l'homme. English]
Manhunts : a philosophical history / Grégoire Chamayou ; translated by Steven Rendall.
  p.   cm.
Includes bibliographical references (p.) and index.
ISBN 978-0-691-15165-6 (alk. paper)
1. Violence–Philosophy. 2. Hunting–Philosophy. 3. Minorities–Crimes against.
4. Lynching. I. Title.
HM886.C4314 2012   303.6–dc232011034778

British Library Cataloging-in-Publication Data is available

Publication of this book has been aided by CNL (Centre national du livre)

This book has been composed in Minion Pro
Printed on acid-free paper. ∞
Printed in the United States of America

1 3 5 7 9 10 8 6 4 2

CONTENTS

MANHUNTS

INTRODUCTION

IN THE FIFTEENTH CENTURY, a very special kind of hunt is said to have taken place in France on the grounds of the royal chateau of Amboise. King Louis XI, who had been offered "the dreadful pleasure of a manhunt," set out in pursuit of a convict wearing the "hide of a freshly killed stag." Released on the grounds and quickly caught by the royal pack of hounds, the man was "torn to pieces by the dogs."[1]

To write a history of manhunts is to write one fragment of a long history of violence on the part of the dominant. It is also to write the history of the technologies of predation indispensable for the establishment and reproduction of relationships of domination.

The manhunt must not be understood here as a metaphor. It refers to concrete historical phenomena in which human beings were tracked down, captured, or killed in accord with the forms of the hunt; these were regular and sometimes large-scale practices whose forms were first theorized in ancient Greece, long before their enormous expansion in the modern period in conjunction with the development of transatlantic capitalism.

The French noun *la chasse* is defined here as "the action of hunting, pursuing, particularly with regard to animals,"[2] but the corresponding verb (*chasser*) also means "chasing out by means of violence or coercion, forcing to leave a certain place." There is a hunt of pursuit and a hunt of expulsion; hunting that captures and hunting that excludes. These two operations are distinct but may enter into a relationship of complementarity: hunting human beings, tracking them down, often presupposes that they have been previously chased out, expelled, or excluded from a common order. Every hunt is accompanied by a theory of its prey that explains why, by virtue of what difference, of what distinction, some men can be hunted and others not. The history of man-hunting is thus a history not only of the techniques of tracking and capture but also of procedures of exclusion, of lines of demarcation drawn within the human community in order to define the humans who can be hunted.

However, the hunter's triumph—and his pleasure—would be less intense if the human hunted were not *nonetheless* a human. The supreme excitement and at the same time the absolute demonstration of social superiority is, in fact, to hunt beings whom one knows to be men and not animals. That is because, as Balzac put it in a formula that can serve here as an axiom, "So the hunt for men is superior to the other class of hunting by all the distance that there is between animals and human beings."[3] Thus, this distance has to be recognized at the same time that it is denied. And therein lies its peculiar challenge: to succeed in erasing the distance between the human hunted and the animal prey, not theoretically but practically, in the act of capture or putting to death. Recognizing the humanity of the prey and at the same time challenging it in practice are thus the two contradictory attitudes constitutive of the manhunt.

If there is an animalization here, it is perhaps in the sense in which Hannah Arendt writes that man "can be fully dominated only when he becomes a specimen of the animal-species man":[4] total domination, a horizon that is difficult to attain, and thus does not involve the animalization of human beings in the sense in which they would cease to be "humans," but rather the reduction of their humanity to *human animality*—an animality that always remains full of its own redoubtable resources.

The main problem has to do with the fact that the hunter and the hunted do not belong to different species. Since the distinction between the predator and his prey is not inscribed in nature, the hunting relationship is always susceptible to a reversal of positions. Prey sometimes band together to become hunters in their turn. The history of a power is also the history of the struggles to overthrow it.

CHAPTER 1

The Hunt for Bipedal Cattle

Man is a tame animal, and I admit that he is hunted.
PLATO, *SOPHIST* 222C

The art of acquiring slaves, I mean of justly acquiring them, . . . [is] a species of hunting or war.
ARISTOTLE, *POLITICS*

A slave . . . has escaped in Alexandria, by name Hermon also called Neilos, by birth a Syrian . . . about 18 years old, of medium stature, beardless, with good legs, a dimple on the chin, a mole by the left side of the nose a scar above the left corner of the mouth, tattooed on the right wrist with two barbaric letters. . . .
    Whoever brings back this slave shall receive 3 talents of copper.
ANONYMOUS PAPYRUS FROM ALEXANDRIA

GREEK PHILOSOPHY contains a warning that political thought has not taken seriously enough, despite the ancients' insistence on it: the masters' power is based on the violent act of capturing their subjects. Domination presupposes a kind of manhunt. This book takes this fundamental thesis as its starting point and examines its implications from the point of view of the dominated, the prey. The goal is to write a history and a philosophy of hunting powers and their technologies of capture.

For the Greeks, the manhunt is not only a metaphor of the play of seduction, hunting for lovers, or sophistical traps. It is

4

also a very literal practice connected with the institution of slavery. The economic life of the city-state is dependent on slave labor, and hence its prior acquisition. Thus, Thucydides tells us that in the course of one of their campaigns the Athenians "captured Hyccara, a small fortified place on the coast which belonged to the Sicanians, but was at war with Egesta. They made slaves of the inhabitants."[1] Battles and military raids were among the main sources of supply for slave labor.

In the *Sophist*, Plato emphasizes the fact that hunting cannot be reduced to tracking wild animals. Among the different branches of the cynegetic art there is also an art of manhunting, which is in turn subdivided into several categories: "Let us define piracy, manstealing, tyranny, the whole military art, by one name, as hunting with violence."[2] Although not all these forms are equally tolerated—for example, Plato condemns piracy, "the chasing of men on the high seas," because it transforms those who practice it into "cruel and lawless hunters"[3]—war appears, by contrast, to be a form of legitimate hunting that is worthy of citizens. Aristotle says much the same: "the art of war is a natural art of acquisition, for the art of acquisition includes hunting, an art which we ought to practice against wild beasts, and against men who, though intended by nature to be governed, will not submit."[4]

Greek philosophers conceive manhunting as an "art" or technology of power. There is an "art of acquiring slaves." From the outset, domination is examined in a technological perspective: what must masters do to be masters? On what procedures does their power depend?

The main characteristic of the manhunt as a technology of power is its nonproductivity: it does not make its object but obtains it by taking it from some external source. According to the classical dichotomy, it is a technology not of production but of acquisition.[5] The Greek seizes his slaves as he would game in the

hunt or fruits in a harvest—that is, without having had to organize the production. It is in this sense that Aristotle can describe
hunting for slaves as a "natural art of acquisition."

But although the manhunt appears to be a technology of
power, it does not figure among the political arts in the full
sense of the term. The cynegetic modality of power is exercised
only as the condition for the master's economic domination. As
such it is not an art of the polis.

The first problem is that of its justification. What authorizes
someone to engage in manhunting?

The question of the legitimacy of capture resonates with
a Greek fear: that of being hunted oneself. The ancient world
was haunted by the menacing specter of the *andrapodistes*,
the manhunter who seized citizens to capture them and sell
them as slaves. Plato, who it is said was himself reduced to
slavery at one point, mentions this danger. Socrates, when
it was suggested that he go into exile in Thessaly, a region
well-known for the activities of its manstealers, refused to
do so, preferring to remain the slave of the laws rather than
risk being the slave of men.[6] This is the theme of the stateless person's insecurity: exile, inasmuch as it is equivalent to
the withdrawal of law, engenders vulnerability. This relation
between the departure from an order of legality and the manhunt firmly places the category of exiles and stateless persons
at the center of the question of relationships of interhuman
predation.

Since free humans, citizens, can be reduced to slavery, how
can we distinguish between legitimate slaves and the others?
Between people who can be hunted and those who cannot?

One solution would be to deny that certain people belong
to humanity, to reduce them to a bestial animality in order to
be able to hunt them. In Greek texts, slaves are regularly *rep-*

resented as nonhumans, but their minimal participation in the species is not contested on the theoretical level. The fact that they are constantly designated by oxymoronic formulas— "bipedal cattle," "living tools"—that simultaneously deny and concede their humanity—seems to make them appear more as *humanoids*:[7] beings in human *form* whose humanity is reduced to that of their bodies. The gap between the slave's nature and the master's is conceived as *analogous*—and not as identical—to the gap that distinguishes humans from animals. According to Aristotle's formula, the distance between slaves and other humans is as great as that "between soul and body, or between men and animals."[8]

What slaves are denied is thus less membership in the human race than participation in the same form of humanity that their masters enjoy. In this view, there are several categories of humans within humanity, each of which is endowed with a different social purpose: some are made to command, others to obey. Slaves by nature, who are capable of understanding reason without being able to exercise it, have to follow the orders of those who possess reason for them. The thesis is well known: there are humans whose bodies dominate their souls. These are slaves by nature. They are also prey by nature.

Slavery is thus inscribed in the ontological status of the dominated, as his natural tendency, which is that of a being-for-domination. However, this nature is merely the master's projection of his will to power, objectified into a theory of the essence of his prey.

The principal objection to this theory resided in the facts: prey by nature stubbornly refused to be what they were supposed to be, resisting their capture and their enslavement.

In the *Laws*, Plato formulates this problem in a way that is original because it is independent of any question of legitimacy:

if slaves are a problem, that is because "the human animal is a kittle [troublesome] beast."[9] The difficulty consists in slaves' particular status as human cattle. Precisely because of this contradictory situation, they do not accept the necessary distinction between free and slave. What is peculiar to humans, we might say, resides in their ability to contest their exclusion from humanity. The solution, a practical one, thus consists in inventorying the technologies that make it possible to maintain this categorial division that the excluded reject. Although Plato does not refer on this occasion to violent capture, from antiquity onward it was nonetheless the first of these political technologies of dividing up the human race.

The case of fugitive slaves or rebellious prey produces a crisis in the order of domination. By escaping and resisting, these slaves are no longer in conformity with their supposed essence. To reestablish the ontological order that has been thus abused, there is ultimately only one recourse: force. Violent hunting will be carried out in the form of war on men who, being born to be commanded, refuse to be commanded. In other words, the only thing left to do is to subjugate by force a prey that does not want to be a prey.

Thus, in the end the answer to the theoretical problem of the manhunt is the practice of manhunting itself, with the paradox that the latter is legitimized on the basis of an allegedly natural division whose nonnaturalness is inseparable from its establishment. In fact, the natural order that is invoked here as the foundation of cynegetic power can be realized only by virtue of a whole arsenal of artifices.

But cynegetic violence does not occur only at the time of the first acquisition, but also later on, as a means of governing. The hunt continues after the capture.

In Sparta, during their long apprenticeship young warriors were sent into the countryside to engage in a hunting party of a special kind, *crypteia*, which Plutarch describes this way: "During the day these young people, spread out in covered places, remained hidden there and rested: when night came, they swept down on the roads and slaughtered whatever helots they could catch. Often they also went into the fields and killed the strongest and the best."[10]

Numerous hypotheses have been proposed to explain this practice: military training, a way of intimidating a slave population that was superior in numbers, a secret police operation to "liquidate" the most dangerous helots, and so on. The historian Jean Ducat emphasizes above all the social and representational function of hunting helots—an initiation rite whose scope extended to the community as a whole: "*cryptia* was like an apprenticeship for—or a representation of—a wild hunt. . . . Every hunt presupposes a prey; the helot, whose special clothing assimilated him to an animal, is that prey." The helot wore a dog-skin cap; the concealed hunter wore a wolf-skin: "In this nocturnal hunt, through a process of inversion that is not absent from rites of passage, it is the animal-prey that captures the animal-hunter, the wild man-beast who brings down the domestic man-animal."[11] The masters' sons turned themselves into beasts of prey to reenact in the present the primal scene of conquest. The arbitrary murder of the helots manifested the truth of power with sanguinary clarity. It was a way of reminding people *who* was the master.

As Thucydides wrote: "Spartan policy with regard to the helots had always been based almost entirely on the idea of security."[12] But a revolt of the helots was less to be feared than a gradual erasure of social borderlines. *Crypteia* was above all intended to remind people of the absolute character of that delimitation. Here, the manhunt appears as a means of *ontological policing*: a violence whose aim is to maintain the dominated in correspondence with their concept, that is, with the concept that the dominant have imposed on them.

At this initial phase, cynegetic violence appears to be the condition, both originary and continuing, of the masters' power. However, as such it remains external to the political sphere of the city-state. It presents itself as the technology of a power, but of an extrapolitical power. On this point, a major conceptual shift was to take place. Much later, in an entirely different horizon of political thought, the motifs of the manhunt and power would combine in a new way.

CHAPTER 2

Nimrod, or Cynegetic Sovereignty

History is stained with the memories of such crimes by these early
kings. War and its conquests is just a kind of manhunt.

J.-J. ROUSSEAU, *ESSAI SUR L'ORIGINE DES LANGUES*

Look at them, they are dreadful and proud; their flaws are part of
their beauty. This one is Nimrod, the man-hunter.

VICTOR HUGO, *NAPOLÉON LE PETIT*

IN GENESIS WE FIND THE STORY OF NIMROD, the son of Chus,
the grandson of Cham, the founder of Babel and the world's first
king: "He was the first on earth to be a mighty man. He was
a mighty hunter before the Lord."[1] This very short passage has
given rise to long interpretations.

In what sense is Nimrod said to be a *hunter*? The commentary in the *Zohar* explains: "By the word *hunter* the Scripture
does not designate a hunter of animals, but a hunter of men."[2]
An exegete adds: "If Nimrod was a hunter properly so called,
this would not concern Moses here; but for him, hunting animals serves as a transition to hunting men; it is in this sense that
he is called 'a mighty hunter'; it is thus that, in a completely opposite case, David is called 'a shepherd of the peoples.' "[3]

After the Flood, God commanded humans to go forth and
populate the Earth. Nimrod disobeyed and brought them to-

FIGURE 1. Nimrod. *Nimbrod Filius Chus*, in Athanasius Kircher, *Turris Babel* (Amsterdam: Janssonius van Waesberg, 1679), p. 112.

gether by force.[4] That is why he is called a hunter of men: in order to become a king, he acquired his subjects by violence. He captured his people.

Nimrod's authority—that of the first sovereign—thus has no foundation other than force. He practiced the abduction of humans, robbed the patriarchs of their authority, and contravened the divine commandment.

In the biblical tradition, the power of the sovereign is thus placed from the outset under the sign of the manhunt. This motif, which the Greeks reserved above all for the analysis of the master's economic power, was to be directly mobilized in the conception of political sovereignty. The theory of the master of slaves and the theory of the hunter-king were superimposed to produce a theory of cynegetic sovereignty.

For example, when Jean Bodin seeks to define *despotic monarchy*, he refers to these two models together: "the first monarchy that ever came into being arose in Assyria, in the time of Nimrod. The Scriptures speak of him as the mighty hunter, which in Hebrew is a common way of referring to a robber. Aristotle and Plato themselves include brigandage as a form of the chase."[5] The king of despotic monarchy is a king-master, whose political sovereignty appears as isomorphic with the master's domination over his slaves.

To the power of tyrannical domination will be opposed power in accord with law, just as voluntary adhesion will be opposed to violent capture. This shift takes place in the modern period, with the development of contractual theories of sovereignty, which did not fail to remember Nimrod.[6] But much earlier, Nimrod had served as a counterpoint to a very different kind of power.

In the Bible, the portrait of the hunter-king is followed by that of Abraham, the shepherd. The contrast is striking. On the one hand, Nimrod, a cruel and idolatrous tyrant; on the other, Abraham, a peaceful and virtuous shepherd. The former, a conquering hunter, glorifies himself, carried away by the passion for domination, while the latter, a humble shepherd, glories only in his obedience to the Lord and his devotion to his flock. The parallel between the two figures becomes a topos of commentary on the Scriptures that is adopted over and over by the vulgate and the preachers: "The first king of Babylon began by being a mighty hunter: the first leader of Israel began by being a shepherd." Whereas "the hunter thinks only of capturing and killing," the shepherd "loves the members of his flock, he knows them; he calls them by their names, he walks in front of them, leads them to good pastures, . . . binds up their wounds, carries them in his arms when they are tired, . . . looks for them everywhere when they have gotten lost; joyfully brings them back on his shoulders, watches over them day and night, risks his life to defend them from the wolves."[7]

What is at stake in the comparison of these two figures goes very far beyond the didactic function of two biblical exempla. In this symmetry and term-for-term opposition are defined two utterly different and incompatible models of political power.

Michel Foucault located, on the basis of Hebrew tradition, the emergence of a pastoral power. But I think this genealogy is missing an essential component. To what, in fact, is the pastorate opposed? In the Old Testament, Foucault explains, "the bad kings, those who are denounced for having betrayed their task, are designated as bad shepherds, not in relation to individuals, but always in reference to the whole."[8] But the figure of the bad king cannot be reduced to the case of the failed shepherd. The real counterpoint to pastoral power, what is opposed to it not simply as a defective form of itself but as its true antithesis, its inverted double and at the same time its foil, is Nimrod, the hunter

of men. In the long history of the thematization of power that
began in Hebrew tradition, there are in fact two opposing terms:
Abraham and Nimrod, pastoral power and cynegetic power.

What are the characteristics of this opposition? The first
principle of pastoral power is its transcendence. God is the supreme shepherd, but he entrusts his flock to subordinate shepherds. The schema is that of the human shepherds' entire dependency and complete submission to divine authority. With
Nimrod the opposite is true: far from receiving his people from
the hand of God, he captures it by force, with his own hands.
The reign of the hunter-king is not only the first power on Earth
but also the first power that is specifically *terrestrial*, whose authority is not inherited from a transcendent source. Nimrod is
the first figure of the immanence of power.[9] His rationality is
that of a physics rather than a theology of power.[10] This is the
first major characteristic of the opposition between cynegetic
power and pastoral power: the immanence of the power relationship or the transcendence of the divine law as the foundation of political authority.

For Foucault, pastoral power was still defined by three other
characteristics: it is exercised over a multiplicity in movement (a
flock); it is fundamentally beneficent (caring for the flock), and
it individualizes its subjects (knowing each member of the flock
individually). A mobile, beneficent, and individualizing power.
Now, as it is presented by tradition, cynegetic power is opposed
term for term to this triple characterization.

Cynegetic power is exercised over prey, living beings that
escape and flee, with a double problem: how to catch them and
how to retain them once they are caught. This power is thus
mobile, but not in the same way as pastoral power. Whereas the
shepherd walks in front of his flock to guide it, the hunter pursues his prey to seize them. But the essential difference does not

lie there. Despite its mobility, cynegetic power remains to a very large extent also a territorial power. While the shepherd knows only a single type of space, that of the pasture, the hunter constantly moves back and forth between two spaces, or more exactly between a *space* and a *territory*: Nimrod is both a hunter and the founder of a city. He reigns over Babel, but he periodically plunges into the space outside to hunt down his prey, which he brings back and piles up inside his walls. His is an urban power, but its exercise is not limited to the circumscribed unit of the city: on the contrary, everything takes place in the relationship between the city's territory and the space outside it, in a movement of annexation that constantly appropriates outside in order to accumulate inside. Although it is deployed on the basis of a territory, Nimrod's power is not limited in its predatory extent by any external boundary. It is exercised, from a territory of accumulation, on the resources of an indefinite exteriority. If Nimrod hunts and builds, that is also because one is the condition of the other: he hunts in order to build. Cynegetic power gathers together what is scattered, centralizes and accumulates it in a limitless logic of annexation. That is the image of Babel: the hunter's accumulation is manifested by a vertical piling-up that will reach even the heavens. The captured people are employed in building the city that imprisons them. The dynamics of cynegetic power is oriented by these two vectors: centralization through the annexation of external resources, and verticalization through the accumulation of captives in the internal territory.

Thus, whereas pastoral power guides and accompanies a multiplicity in movement, cynegetic power extends itself, on the basis of a territory of accumulation, over a space of capture. Whereas pastoral power is fundamentally beneficent, cynegetic power is essentially predatory. If the shepherd Moses was chosen as the political shepherd of the people of Israel, that is because he had demonstrated, through his aptitude for guiding flocks, qualities that could be transferred to the government of people. In contrast, as John of Salisbury wrote, "The arrogance of the tyrant . . . had no other founder than he who learned to scorn the Lord by slaughtering wild animals and rolling in their blood."[11] Just as pastoral power prepares for good government, hunting is the school of tyranny. Whereas pastoral power is governed by a managing rationality of the growth of internal resources, cynegetic power imposes a logic of raids or levies. In the medieval imagination, Nimrod is the symbol of fiscal power: "When he could capture a man or a woman, before he let them go he made them promise to hand over every year, to him or to his heir, an ox or a certain amount of wheat."[12] While the shepherd is concerned with the life and the health of his subjects, the hunter taxes and consumes, if necessary to the point of exhausting and even killing his subjects.

Finally, whereas pastoral power is an individualizing power—in the sense in which the shepherd has to give individual attention to each of his sheep—cynegetic power, although it proceeds by division, does so with a view to accumulation. The hunt begins by scattering the group of prey in order to isolate the most vulnerable. This is a process of division: separating the individual from his group. But if this process first isolates its prey, it is only the better to massify them again afterward. In a monumental inscription, King Ashurbanipal "prides himself on having killed with his own hands no less than 450 great lions, 390 wild bulls, mounted on his chariot, also to have cut the heads off 200 ostriches, caught 30 elephants in traps and seized, alive, 50 wild bulls, 140 ostriches, and 20 large lions."[13] Cynegetic power accumulates; it does not individualize.

Because it has to labor for the salvation of its subjects, pastoral power is caught in a dialectic of the whole and the part, with the dilemmas this entails: can one sacrifice one sheep to save the rest of the flock? No such question arises for cynegetic power:

they can all die. In the event of losses, it can always seek further
resources outside. This power is not governed by any imperative
of preservation. Consequently, for cynegetic power there is no
choice to be made as to who shall survive and who not; there is
no problematics of sacrifice.

Christianity continues this opposition between pastoral
power and cynegetic power, which it uses chiefly to distinguish
between the spiritual and the temporal modalities of governing
humans.

The Gospels say: "As he walked by the Sea of Galilee, he saw
two brothers, Simon who is called Peter and Andrew his brother,
casting a net into the sea; for they were fishermen. And he said
unto them, 'Follow me, and I will make you fishers of men.' Immediately they left their nets and followed him."[14] Christian
proselytizing finds here one of its great metaphors: fishing for
men. To gather together its faithful, Christianity does not hunt;
it fishes.

Hobbes comments: "And [regeneration] is compared by our
Saviour, to Fishing, that is, to winning men to obedience, not by
Coercion, and Punishing, but by Perswasion. Therefore he said
not to his Apostles, hee would make them so many Nimrods,
Hunters of Men; but Fishers of Men."[15] Strict persuasion is opposed to the right of coercion. Thus, in this tradition the sovereign's political power is distinguished from the strictly spiritual
power of the Church.[16]

What emerges with the story of Nimrod is a forgotten continent
of Western political thought. If Foucault could say that beginning with the rise of Hebrew, and then Christian, pastoralism,
politics has been largely considered a matter of the sheepfold,[17]
we can add that it was also, though in accord with a parallel and
opposed genealogy, a matter of hunting.

CHAPTER 3

Diseased Sheep and Wolf-Men

> If the consequences of this terrible faith were cruel, we have to agree
> that they were logical. A king is a shepherd of men, and the shepherd
> must cure the diseased sheep or kill it, to avoid seeing his whole flock
> infected.
>
> EUGÈNE MOUTON, *LES LOIS PÉNALES DE LA FRANCE*

> The word *wargus* meant wolf and robber, because the exile, just like
> the beast of prey, is an inhabitant of the forest, and like the wolf, may
> be killed with impunity.
>
> JACOB GRIMM, *DEUTSCHE RECHTSALTERTHUEMER*

IN 1329, SIMON ROLAND OF CARCASSONNE, suspected of being still "infected with heretical errors that have been so often
condemned by the authority of the popes," was brought to trial
before the Inquisition. The phrases he heard when he was sen-
tenced had no doubt been uttered by his judges dozens of times
before: "We, Pilfort, bishop of Pamiers by the grace of God, . . .
fearing that, like a diseased sheep, you might infect the other
sheep in the flock, . . . declare you an obstinate heretic, and as
such we deliver you to the secular authorities."[1]

Christian pastoralism was opposed, as we have seen, to cynegetic power: fishing for souls rather than hunting for men,
persuasion rather than coercion. Pastoral power was defined as

an antihunting. However—and this is the paradox—it developed its own cynegetic practices, its own forms of manhunts, *pastoral hunts*.

What fundamentally distinguished the pastoral model from the cynegetic model, and what radically forbade the former to entertain any predatory relationship, was the imperative of caring and protecting. A protective power versus a predatory power: that was the line of opposition. But pastoral hunting took place precisely in the name of protecting the flock. To protect the flock sometimes one has to hunt down certain sheep, to sacrifice a few to save all the others. Here we are no longer in a logic of predatory appropriation but rather in a rationality of salutary ablation and beneficent exclusion.

From the divine imperative "you shall lead my flock to pasture" followed several prerogatives for pastoral power: "Every shepherd," Cardinal Bellarmine wrote, "must have three sorts of power to defend his flock: a power over wolves, to prevent them from killing his ewes; a power over the rams, to prevent them from harming the ewes; and a power over the sheep in general, to give them the necessary pasturage. Thus, if one of the princes of the flock changes into a ram or a wolf, mustn't the vicar of Christ have the power to drive him away?"[2]

The favorite image for pastoral hunting in order to exclude is health-related: metaphors of illness, gangrene, or epidemics. It is necessary to prevent the infection from spreading, to forestall general contagion. According to St. Jerome, "the gangrenous flesh must be cut away, and the diseased sheep must be driven far from the fold, for fear that the mass of blood, the individual, the household as a whole, and the whole flock might be invaded."[3]

To this imagery correspond techniques for identifying, excluding, and eliminating dangerous elements, as well as a the-

FIGURE 2. The Church devouring its flock (1539). Frontispice in Urbanus Rhegius, *Wie man die falschen Propheten erkennen, ja greiffen mag* (Wittenberg: n.p., 1539).

ory of the diseased sheep and the corresponding practices of investigation, excommunication, and burning at the stake. The great task of the Inquisition consisted in identifying heretical individuals. This involved unprecedented activities of surveillance and control, a whole archival apparatus. This was again the case, at the threshold of modernity, with the great witch hunts: "The essential process in combating witchcraft was discovering who the witches were rather than where they were located.

Witch-hunting involved the identification of individuals who were engaged in a secret or occult activity."[4] When it turns to hunting, pastoral power diverts to repressive ends the whole set of delicate procedures of individualization that were originally intended to help care for the subjects involved.

Because they are directed against members of the community, pastoral hunts imply an act of exclusion: excommunication, which deprives the believer of the sacraments, of the right to enter the church, to participate in the communion of prayer inside it and in the society of the faithful outside it. But the excommunicated individual is not merely chased away from the flock. The protection of his shepherd having been withdrawn from him, he is exposed to all kinds of predations, abandoned to a physical and spiritual death "just as someone who threw a sheep out of its fold or its shed at night would be judged to have thrown it into the jaws of the wolves."[5]

This is an important point: unlike acquisition hunts, pastoral exclusion hunts tend to eliminate the subjects concerned. It is less a matter of capturing prey than of doing away with animals that have become dangerous. Christian theology is quite clear on this point, at least in the case of St. Thomas: heretics, he writes, deserve "not only to be separated from the Church by excommunication, but even to be removed from the world by death."[6] The diseased sheep will thus be handed over "to the secular judge so that he can make him disappear from the number of the living." But what is the foundation for this right to kill? The evangelical doctor establishes it by means of the analogy to the prince's right to execute counterfeiters: the heretic also falsifies the authentic and puts the false into circulation. Still graver, by counterfeiting dogma he challenges the ecclesiastical monopoly on issuing truths. In so doing he undermines authority. And for that he must be eliminated. Let us note that this connection between the pastoral management of subjects, the monopoly on the production of truth, and the power of exclusion continued to function long afterward, beyond the strictly ecclesiastical context, in a whole series of institutions—political parties, states, and organizations, all of which function in the mode of dogma, exclusion, and purges.

Exclusion hunts are not peculiar to religious powers. Sovereigns have also long banished and proscribed.

In ancient Nordic and Germanic law, one who has been banished is put literally "outside the law." As a result of this exclusion from the legal order, he thus became the prey of a popular search. Anyone can kill them with impunity. The Anglo-Saxon *Utlag* and the Scots *out-law* is also called, in Icelandic, a wolf, *Vargr*, "to signify that being excluded from the society of men, he was reduced to wandering in the forests like a wild beast." The outcast who remained in the territory was described "as the wolf in the sanctuary . . . [and] he was represented with a wolf's head."[7]

The wolf is a ferocious beast that threatens the flock; if the outcast is assimilated to a wolf, that is because, like the wolf, he has to be killed. As Robert Jacob wrote, "the language of the law thus indicates that in its view, he [the outcast] has become a harmful animal, whose physical liquidation is not only not punishable but even recommended."[8]

In the countryside, old shepherd dogs sometimes return to the forest and begin to attack livestock. Once having tasted blood, they are transformed into predators. Then they must be killed. It is this experience of metamorphosis, which is familiar to pastoral societies, that mobilizes the penal image of the wolf-man. The myth of the werewolf is rooted in the same source. But although it probably echoes age-old practices, historians point out that this vocabulary began to make major inroads in the language of law only in the twelfth century,[9] under the influence of Christian pastoralism.

Historically, the penal exclusion of the exile is threefold: exclusion from the community, from the law, and from security.

First, exclusion from the community. As in cases of religious excommunication, the condemned individual is expelled from the human community. This is shunning. The measure concerns not only the proscribed person but also, along with him, the whole community, which is forbidden, on pain of sanctions, to entertain any relationship with him. Speaking to the banished person, offering him hospitality, feeding him, constitute, even and especially for those close to him, crimes: Salic law stipulates that "anyone . . . who has given him bread or shelter, even if it is his wife or a close relative, shall be judged guilty."[10] All solidarity is prohibited.

Then, the exclusion from the law. Chased out of social relationships, the exile is also chased outside the law: "We withdraw from you any right of country and we put you in complete nonlaw," stipulated some formulas of banishment.[11] The banished person is put outside the law, *illegalized*.

Finally, the exclusion from security. The condemned person is put *outside the sovereign's word*, excluded from the *sermo regis*, the oath of protection binding the sovereign to his subjects.[12] This loss of the sovereign's protection abandons the subject to a radical insecurity: "We hand over . . . your body and your flesh to the beasts of the forests, to the birds in the sky, and the fish that live in the waters; we permit anyone to disturb your peace and your security anywhere where others have the right to enjoy them, and we send you to the four corners of the Earth."[13] Being exposed to natural predation is the exact counterpart of the security promised by the political oath. But the banished person is not simply an "undefended" individual left to the mercy of those whom he encounters; he is even positively designated as an enemy that may be killed, as a life that can be taken without committing a crime: "We put him outside our word, so that anyone who meets him may kill him with impunity,"[14] a sixth-century edict issued by Chilperic promises. Beyond a simple descent back into a natural vulnerability, this involves an active policy of making the individual vulnerable. The hunt has begun.

Dead to society, dead to the law, dead to the state, the proscribed man sees his wife declared a widow and his children orphans. He also knows that he will eventually be denied burial "in order to erase every trace of his stay on Earth."[15] Society, which struck him with anathema by assimilating him to the beasts of the forest, "no longer recognized him as one of its members, not even as a man; or at least, it considered him fictively as deprived of life."[16] He became one of the walking dead.

In later periods, we find again these procedures of fictive putting to death—in a very spectacular form in the "executions by effigy" that accompanied civil condemnations to death in early modern times. In the seventeenth century, when a condemned man was absent and could not be executed, his image was killed instead: "It was fine to see, on the square where executions took place, so many pictures displayed in each of which an executioner cut off a head. . . . [T]he whole people came out of curiosity to see this crowd of painted criminals who constantly died and did not die at all. . . . This is an invention that the judicial system has found to defame those whom it cannot punish, and to chastise the crime when it does not hold the criminal."[17]

But these forms of social, legal, and symbolic death serve above all as adjuncts to hunting. In a kind of smoking-out by social and legal dispossession, the goal is chiefly to deprive the fugitive of being able to breathe the air of society and law, to cut him off from his escape route in order to flush him out. This procedure is particularly clear in the case of condemnation in absentia, where "putting outside the law the accused or the defender who escapes justice is less a punishment than a means of coercion that tends to lead him to turn himself in."[18] A paradoxical tactic that consists in expelling absent subjects in order to find them again. Not being able to lay hands on the fugitive, not being able to imprison him, society closes itself to him, in what Robert Jacob has described as a "kind of inverted penitentiary system in which society imprisons itself while the delinquent runs free."[19]

But sometimes, when their numbers increase, the proscribed gather together to form bands in the forest. The banished become bandits. Confronted by this threat, a hunt is organized to track down the outcasts as if they were wild beasts: a bounty is put on their heads and rewards are promised to those who bring in their remains. In Iceland, it was, it is said, a *Logmadr* by the name of Lylulf-Valdergarson who thought up this "heroic and barbaric way of getting rid of these kinds of beasts of the forest, whom despair and hunger led to commit all kinds of crimes. At his suggestion, a price was put on the head of each of the proscribed."[20] There was even a time at the end of the thirteenth century "when a bounty for killing or a tenth of brandy was offered to anyone who brought to the county court the head of a wolf or a banished outcast."[21]

For Giorgio Agamben, the figure of the outcast reveals something essential and hidden about the essence of political sovereignty: "This lupinization of man and humanization of the wolf is at every moment possible in the *dissolutio civitatis* inaugurated by the state of exception."[22] Contrary to what socialcontract theories claim, the state of nature is not anterior to the political order, it is not transcended by the latter but is, on the contrary, a virtuality within it that can always be reactivated in the mode of the exception to the law. Whereas the sovereign power claims to exercise itself on legal subjects, in reality its object is "naked life," which is usually masked by the showy garb of legal personality, but which proscription brings to light in its absolute nakedness.

There is another way of interpreting the political significance of hunting wolf-men, however. Rather than seeing in them a manifestation of sovereign omnipotence, Eric Hobsbawm shows, on the contrary, that these practices of banishment—the institution from which "bandits" take their name—testifies instead to the "shallowness of the power system. Everybody was entitled to kill the outlaw, because nobody was in a position to apply their law to him."[23] Banishment, then, appears as the sign of a weak power that is incapable of catching the fugitive, a step taken in the absence of the offender, an expedient of power confronted by subjects who escape it.

By permitting everyone to attack the fugitive, the sovereign also fell into a dangerous contradiction: authorizing someone to kill the condemned man was equivalent to delegating the sovereign's prerogatives to the mass of the people—that is, de facto, renouncing the sovereign's monopoly on legitimate violence. This contradiction, which is characteristic of a sovereignty that is not fully developed, was to be overcome—partially—only with the establishment of modern state apparatuses endowed with organized police forces. Proscriptions faded away historically in precise proportion to the growing strength of the police state.

The political secret that was betrayed by hunts for wolf-men is that, historically, sovereign power was relatively powerless.

The slave-master's acquisition hunts, tyrannical sovereignty's capture hunts, pastoral power's exclusion hunts: thus, at the dawn of modernity there were three well-defined forms of cynegetic power. A new historical experience was soon to require a revision of these old models.

CHAPTER 4

Hunting Indians

They hunted down the natives with dogs. These wretched savages, almost naked and without arms, were pursued like wild beasts in a forest, devoured alive by dogs, shot to death.

VOLTAIRE, *ESSAI SUR LES MOEURS*

In Europe, we do not know what a war with savages is like. Hunting down men with dogs is still nothing; but these are wars of extermination.

ANONYMOUS, *COUP D'OEIL SUR LA SOCIÉTÉ ET LES MOEURS DES ÉTATS-UNIS D'AMÉRIQUE*

THE SPANISH CHRONICLE recounts the exploits of Leoncico, the faithful companion of the conquistador Vasco Núñez de Balboa: "Leoncico, from the dog Becerrico, of the island of St Juan, and no less famous than his parent."[1] Having a right to the same portion of the booty as his human comrades, he brought his master more than two thousand gold pesos. Oviedo describes his ruddy coat and his robust body, marked with countless scars received in combat: "When the Spaniards were taking or pursuing the Indians, on loosing this animal, and saying, 'There he is—seek him,' he would commence the chase, and had so fine a scent, that they scarcely ever escaped him. And when he had overtaken his object, if the Indian remained quiet, he would take him by the sleeve, or hand, and lead him gently, without biting or annoying him, but if he resisted, he would tear him in pieces."[2] More than three centuries later, a French missionary in America was still able to praise such animals with enthusiasm, describing a "greyhound that had been admirably trained to hunt Indians, and was no less remarkable for his beauty than for his intelligence."[3]

The conquest of the New World gave rise to vast manhunts that continued for almost four centuries and took place all over the Americas—hunts to enslave and hunts to kill. This was a massive phenomenon with its specially trained dogs, professional hunters, weapons, and culture.

In South America, where slave-hunting persisted for a long time after the initial conquest, whole cities specialized in this economic activity. For more than three centuries, the residents of São Paulo—the *Paulistas*—had as almost their sole source of revenue the occupation they called *descer indios*, tracking down Indians.[4] These *bandeirantes* at the head of small armed groups carried out attacks on autochthonous tribes in order to capture them and sell them as slaves. They caught tens of thousands of natives. Among the most famous of the Paulist leaders was a certain João Amaro, who at the end of the seventeenth century commanded a band of "*Mamalucos* trained in the art of man-hunting."[5] The *mamalucos* are described as having "shot and powder, some carrying a gun, others a bow and arrows, and all of them armed with a long knife . . . , barefoot, with a leather belt around their loins and a wide-brimmed straw hat on their heads, without any other clothing except crude cotton trousers and a short shirt whose tails floated over the trousers, sometimes a breastplate and thigh-guards made of stag's leather."[6]

As a social phenomenon, Indian hunting was indissolubly a large-scale economic activity, a way of life, and a cruel pleasure, a macabre form of sport—and this was so from the beginning of the conquests, when it clearly appeared that "it was not only to use them as beasts of burden that the Spaniards hunted them; it was also a pastime and a way of occupying their leisure time."[7]

Acquisition hunts were intended to take future slaves. These were capture hunts. The prey was not to be killed—or rather, some of it was to be left alive. Extermination hunts were entirely different; their main goal was the eradication of the population in order to conquer the territory. It was not only disease that decimated the native populations of the Americas, but also a policy of extreme violence that sought to destroy them. In the nineteenth century, Schoolcraft, who reports that in North America Indians were killed "as people go to hunt wild beasts," quotes a supervisor of Indian affairs who solemnly declared that the whites were waging "a war of extermination against the Indians."[8]

In 1725, the government of Massachusetts had encouraged private individuals to engage in the lucrative activity of murder. It had set a bounty of a hundred pounds for every Indian scalp.[9] A certain Lovewell, who had put himself at the head of a company of volunteers, won a few successes before he met an evil end, dying as he had lived:

> On May 8, he saw an Indian on a point of land that projected into a lake. . . . Without moving, the Indian let himself be approached, even though he was in certain danger of death. When Lovewell had arrived within gunshot range, the Indian shot at him and wounded him, and, receiving a volley himself, he died pierced by several shots. At the same time, 80 Indians who had been hidden in the brush seized groups of Englishmen and fell upon them in turn, with their tomahawks or hatchets; they killed seven of them. . . . This affair put an end to these barbarous excursions.[10]

But only temporarily.

When Charles Darwin visited Santa Fe, Argentina, more than a century later, he discovered that the favorite occupation of the governor was to "hunt Indians. A short time before, he had massacred forty-eight of them and sold their children."[11]

Manhunting had probably never been so widespread, being pursued on a continental scale and resulting in enormous massacres.

These hunts of conquest had to be provided with legitimations, with theories. How could the hunts for Indians be justified? That is where, very early on, philosophers made their entrance.

Following Aristotle, as early as the sixteenth century some philosophers tried to develop a theory of just war based on a conception of the nature of the Indians, that is, on an anthropology. How in fact can you justify a war against a people that has *done* nothing to you, if not on the basis of what they *are*? I have already mentioned that every manhunt presupposes a theory of its prey. This was also the case here.

When the Spanish humanist Juan Ginés de Sepúlveda undertook to ground in reason the enslavement of the Indian populations, he quite naturally referred to Aristotle, whose works he had spent a large part of his life translating and annotating. He remembered in particular the famous passage about slaves by nature and hunting as a branch of the art of war. The Indians, he wrote, "are barbarous and inhuman peoples, foreign to civil life and to peaceful customs. And it will always be just and in conformity with natural law that these people be subjected to the rule of more cultivated and humane princes and nations, so that, benefiting from their virtues and the wisdom of their laws, they might move away from barbarity and decide to take up a more humane way of life. . . . However, if they reject such rule, the latter may be imposed on them by force of arms, and this war will be just according to natural law."[12] He goes on to cite Aristotle: there is an "art of hunting that it is appropriate to use not only against animals, but also against humans who, being born to obey, refuse servitude." What had for a long time been only a dormant formula abandoned to the dust of monasteries now came back to life, in the most concrete way, on the other side of the Atlantic. The manhunt was back, and with it came the old doctrines.

But this readoption of ancient theories took place within an entirely different philosophical horizon, that of Christian humanism. This did not proceed without hitches, however. The strongest tension emerged when the Aristotelian theory of domination came into contact with the Christian doctrine of conversion. Whereas the former was based on a differential and fixed conception of inequality, the latter professed officially a dogma of the unity of the human race and of universal equality.

Conscious of the difficulty, Sepúlveda tried a reconciliation that took the form of a significant revision of Aristotle's thesis. His contribution consisted in this: the subjection of humans of lesser humanity will henceforth take place not only on the pretext of the imperfection of their nature but also with a view to their *humanization*. Through its dynamic dimension, this argument in terms of civilizing clashed with the old theory of the slave by nature. Similarly, war-hunting, which in Aristotle was a simple means of acquisition that left the nature of its prey unchanged, was henceforth presented as a means of humanizing them. This claim was made—more than a little paradoxically—even though it amounted in practice to treating the prey as animals.

But Sepúlveda seemed to hesitate. First of all, the Indians were described as *homunculi*, literally little men, diminished men, "in whom we find hardly a trace of humanity"[13]—an imperfection that made them incapable of governing themselves, and consequently provided the foundation for Europeans' right, as more human, to rule over them. It was the argument based on the superior humanity of the conqueror.[14] But Sepúlveda had hardly set forth this thesis of the natives' deficient humanity before he moved on to another, that of their *moral inhumanity*: they "ate human flesh,"[15] they practiced "monstrous rites with the sacrifice of human victims"[16]—crimes against nature whose enormity excluded their perpetrators from the ranks of humanity. A radical exclusion that did not, however, prevent Sepúlveda from recognizing a few paragraphs later that these natives had a human essence, as soon as it was a question of showing that conquest was the privileged instrument for propagating the Christian faith—one cannot evangelize beasts.

"Hardly human," "inhuman," "humans"—the qualifiers vary completely depending on whether it is a matter of recognizing that the Indians are imperfectly human in order to dominate them, perfectly inhuman in order to proscribe them, or essentially human in order to convert them. But in reality this ontological hesitation only translated philosophically the threefold power relationship that was to be applied to the Indians in practice: that of the slave-master, the sovereign, and the shepherd. The problem was that these different forms of power, even though in America they were in the process of fusing in practice, were historically endowed with heterogeneous discourses of legitimation. To provide a theoretical justification for the new right of conquest, these different discourses had to be integrated into a coherent whole.

These elements, which were at first weakly connected, later merged in a unified theory of colonial power. The latter was magisterially formulated by Francis Bacon in 1622, in his *An*

Advertisement Touching a Holy War.[17] He puts it in the mouth of Zebedaeus, a "zealous Roman Catholic" who incarnates the positions of Catholic fundamentalism at the time.

Not surprisingly, everything begins with Aristotle: "from the very nativity some things are born to rule, and some things to obey."[18] But this classic thesis is immediately reformulated in juridico-theological terms. What is it that allows us to deny the right of a people to govern itself? To answer this question, one has to "go back to the original donation of government,"[19] that is, to the Bible, which offers in a single sentence the key to the foundation of sovereignty: "Let us make man after our own image, and let him have dominion over the fishes of the sea, and the fowls of the air, and the beasts of the land " (Genesis 1:26).[20] Bacon/Zebedaeus, following Francisco de Vitoria, thinks these two ideas—man in the image of God and man's dominion over the Earth—are logically connected: "Domination is founded only in the image of God."[21] Because of this iconic theory of sovereignty, it suffices that men depart from the divine resemblance for them to lose all power. The *imago dei* is the condition of the right to sovereignty: "Deface the image, and you divest the right."[22] But how can we recognize this defacement? The image of God has "natural reason" as its equivalent. "Defaced" people are, thus, those whose way of life diverges from reasonable norms of life. Such a divergence leads not only to the loss of their sovereignty, but also to their being excluded by other nations: "By this we may see, that there are nations in name, that are no nations in right, but multitudes only, and swarms of people. For like as there are particular persons outlawed and proscribed by civil laws of several countries; so are there nations that are outlawed and proscribed by the law of nature."[23]

Here we see the connection of the two notions that up to this point we have encountered only in the mode of juxtaposition.

In Sepúlveda, on the one hand the Indians correspond to the concept of the slave by nature, and on the other hand they are excluded from the common law because of the inhumanity of their customs. Here, it is the divergence from the image of God, *sive* from natural law, that becomes the very content of a revised concept of the slave by nature. The two notions are tied together in such a way that the first is now defined by the second: those who are servile by nature are those who diverge from the theologico-juridical definition of human nature—a disharmony that puts them outside the law.

Slaves and exiles, the dominated and the proscribed, outlaws and the subjugated: these categories, which are heir to two distinct systems of political rationality, were in the process of fusing. But once again, this conceptual reforging expressed the combination of factually corresponding practices: hunting slaves and hunting wolf-men, hunting to acquire and hunting to exclude, hunting to dominate and hunting to eradicate were all combined in the conquest of the New World.

This categorial synthesis corresponded to the construction of a new concept of prey that extended to peoples to be conquered the notion of "common enemies of the human race," which had previously been reserved for pirates. This was an act of *proscribing the enemy*, who was identified with nations contrary to nature.[24] The Indians, because they were cannibals, had made "it lawful for the Spaniards to invade their territory, forfeited by the law of nature; and either to reduce them or displant them."[25] The schema of pastoral exclusion was reappropriated, but it was expanded to the global scale to make it the theoretical matrix of a universal hunt for peoples proscribed from humanity.

At the end of this process of redefinition, the prey is considered less inferior by nature than naturally outside the law. If the first characterization authorizes the prey's subjugation, the second requires its eradication. Refounded on such a basis, nascent imperialism received an absolute, de jure power of hostility that might limit itself to conquest but could also go so far as massacre.

Zebedaeus's speech ended with an appeal for a military coalition of civilized nations: "We Christians, unto whom it is revealed . . . that two singular persons were the parents from whom all the generations of the world are descended: we, I say, ought to acknowledge, that no nations are wholly aliens and strangers the one to the other." Citing Terence—"I am a man and nothing human is foreign to me"—Zebedaeus continues: "if there be such a tacit league or confederation, sure it is not idle; . . . it is against such routs and shoals of people, as have utterly degenerated from the laws of nature; as have in their very body and frame of estate a monstrosity; and may be truly accounted, . . . common enemies and grievances of mankind; or disgraces and reproaches to human nature. Such people, all nations are interested, and ought to be resenting, to suppress."[26]

The text surprises us not only by its violence but also because it seems to involve a contradiction in terms: appealing to fundamental maxims of humanism in order to found a call for the military subjugation of peoples who have degenerated from humanity. This raises the problem of the relationship between humanism and the manhunt, since the latter is now fully justified in this vocabulary.

Carl Schmitt has tried to show that this tension is only apparent. People were in the process of making the transition, in the theory of just war, from an argument derived from a particular concept of humanity (the superior humanity of the conqueror, an argument of Aristotelian inspiration), to a different argument: that of the conqueror's absolute humanity, proclaimed to the exclusion of that of his enemies, who are henceforth seen as inhuman and susceptible to be subjected to unlimited violence.[27] For Schmitt, humanism is in itself the bearer of a murderous exclusion: "Pufendorf . . . quotes approvingly Bacon's comment that specific peoples are 'proscribed by nature itself,' e.g., the Indians, because they eat human flesh. And in fact the Indians of North America were then exterminated."[28]

In *The Nomos of the Earth*, Schmitt went further, adding, apropos of Sepúlveda and Bacon, that "by no means is it paradoxical that none other than humanists and humanitarians put forward such inhuman arguments."[29] He thinks "humanitarian ideology" has a "force of discriminating scission" by virtue of which the political invocation of the human necessarily implies the designation of an inhuman as its hostile double. Fighting in the name of humanity would thus necessarily presuppose the dehumanization of one's enemies, in a logic that leads to extermination.

But Schmitt's underlying thesis consisted, in fact, in the claim, which adopts in a subtle way an old theme of the reactionary criticism of the Enlightenment borrowed from his teacher Donoso Cortes, to the effect that "the pseudo-religion of absolute humanity paved the way for inhuman terrorism."[30] Paradoxically, it would be humanism's universalist ideology that led to the massacre of the Indians and that became the matrix of all the later genocidal logics, for which it would ultimately bear the historical responsibility. A way of turning the argument against the sender and at the same time cleansing nationalism and racism of their own murderous tendencies—a theme which, developed in 1950 by a former Nazi, assumes all its historical significance. Schmitt's tactical cleverness consists in disguising his traditional reactionary critique of humanism as a critique of imperialism— the massacre of the Indians, here presented as a logical outcome of "humanitarian ideology," is supposed to provide an initial historical confirmation of his thesis.

However, apart from the fact that his analysis is marred by anachronism—in fact, neither Sepúlveda nor the character that

Bacon dramatizes in the role of a "zealous Catholic" can be in any way assimilated to the proponents of a secularized philosophy of absolute humanity[31]—Schmitt commits a significant error: contrary to what he claims, Pufendorf, far from saying that Bacon/Zebedaeus is right, explicitly contradicts him: "Neither can I approve of what is said by the famous Bacon, chancellor of England, that a custom like that of the Americans, who sacrifice humans to their false divinities, and who eat human flesh, is a sufficient reason to declare war on these peoples, as on people proscribed by Nature."[32] More interesting is the reason for Pufendorf's refusal. Barbeyrac, commenting on Pufendorf's text, explains it in the following way: if Pufendorf rejects the argument founded on the inhumanity of the enemy's customs, that is because he "here tacitly excludes from the number of legitimate causes for war the punishment of criminal actions that do no harm to oneself."[33] What was at issue was thus not so much Christian humanism, the general horizon shared—as we shall see—by all the main participants in the debate in this period, than the extension of a certain penal logic to the law of war.

In the works of Sepúlveda and Bacon, the universalism of Christian humanism served to generalize to the global scale forms of proscription that had been elaborated within the penal power, in order to lay the foundations for an imperial sovereignty presented as humanity's police: the enemy was presented as a criminal, and war was justified to punish him. But the problem involved in criminalizing the enemy in the theory of war was thereby connected back to that of the proscription of the outlaw, to his dehumanization in the mechanisms of sovereign exclusion. For that reason, the criminalization of the enemy cannot be subjected to a radical critique without a preliminary critique of the way penal philosophy makes the exile an enemy. If humanism has been able to serve as a justification for dehumanizing the condemned, historically it has also served as a basis for the critique of punishment, beginning with capital punishment, by opposing to the dehumanization of the condemned his imprescriptible humanity as a person. It is precisely such conflictual uses of the concept of humanity that Schmitt tends to elude by arguing as if humanistic discourse had been reduced to its imperialist component. This kind of amalgam is probably necessary for the political demonstration he intends to conduct, but it leads him—and this is the chief point—to mutilate the dialectic of humanism that he recognizes elsewhere and to provide merely a truncated version of it that is incapable of taking into account the complexity of its historical uses.

When Las Casas contradicts Sepúlveda,[34] refusing to describe Indians as "animals deprived of human reason, which one has the right to hunt and which can be flushed out like wild animals,"[35] he also does so—but probably more consistently—in the name of the principles of Christian humanism:

Christ wanted his sole precept to be called "charity," and it is owed to all without exception: "Here there cannot be Greek and Jew, circumcised and uncircumcised, barbarian, Scythian, slave, free man, but Christ is all, and in all.'—Consequently, although the philosopher [Aristotle], not knowing Christian truth and charity, writes that the wisest man can hunt down barbarians as though they were wild beasts, we absolutely do not see why barbarians should be killed or subjected, like mules, to an exhausting, cruel, painful, and difficult labor, and to that end be hunted and captured by the wisest man. Let us ignore Aristotle, for we have received from Christ who is eternal truth the following mandate: "Love thy neighbor as thyself."[36]

According to Las Casas, humanity is no longer an essential attribute that can be monopolized (we are the only true humans) but an unconditional principle of conduct associated with the principle of charity: in order to embody humanity, it does not suffice to *be* human; one has to *act* human as well.[37] Thus, far from appearing as an exclusive determination, humanity is defined dialectically by the rejection of this exclusion: an inhuman person is one who excludes other humans from humanity. It is because of this relational redefinition that the political mobilization of the concept of humanity leads here to consequences diametrically opposed to the earlier ones.[38] The theoretical and practical dehumanization of the enemy is thus one of the possible political *uses* of the concept of humanity, but it is not the only one.

Hence it was not "humanism" that led, by a kind of logical necessity, to the massacre—and the proof of this is that "humanism" was just as much opposed to it. The fact that "humanity" is a political concept with contradictory powers is precisely what gives it all its historical interest. It also explains why this concept could be used by both sides in the debate over the colonization of the Americas, both by proponents of violent conquest who called for hunting down the Indians in the name of humanity and by the defenders of the Indians who condemned such hunting in the name of humanity.

Unless we lapse into the idealism of the concept, we have to view humanism as what it is and was, that is, not as a unified subject of history, but as an arena of debate, a common language within which contradictory positions could be formulated. This is not, moreover, a great discovery: the same discourse can be used and completely reversed on both sides of the front lines, and take on, depending on the forces that make use of it, contradictory political meanings. Merleau-Ponty reminds us of the episode during the slave rebellion in Santo Domingo in which Napoleon's troops, who had come to crush the rebellion, heard the insurgents singing the French revolutionary song "Ça ira" on the other side of the wall. Two camps opposed to each other in a battle to the death sang the same song. A way of saying that concepts or "values" cannot be evaluated in abstraction from the people who represent them, and that their political effects cannot be deduced analytically from their definition but are at stake in a reinterpretation by the forces that are involved in the conflict[39] and whose confrontation alone confers on these concepts their political meaning, that is, their *position*. Methodologically, this implies that one must not stop at the abstract analysis of principles but learn to discern their uses and to choose the people "with whom society is to be made."

That is precisely what Schmitt, amalgamating and not differentiating, *pretends* not to know. Consequently, his analysis prohibits us from taking into account not only the fact that there are multiple versions of political humanism but also the complex interplay of conflictual reappropriation to which this discourse can give rise. The reduction of universalism to its imperialist aspect seeks in fact to exclude—and this has always been the goal of reactionary critics—its emancipatory uses.

Expressing and conceiving the enormous manhunts in the New World thus required that all three of the major traditional motifs of cynegetic power be conjoined: the Indians were simultaneously *acquired* as slaves, *subjugated* as subjects, and *proscribed* as outlaws.

But far from being a logical consequence of a univocal political humanism, these violent acts were, much more prosaically, a manifestation—not the only one, as we will see—of a vast and brutal process of economic appropriation, of a burning thirst for gold and conquest. At the same time, on the other side of the Atlantic, other hunts had begun. They had the same motivations.

CHAPTER 5

Hunting Black Skins

The discovery of gold and silver in America, the extirpation, enslavement and entombment in mines of the aboriginal population, . . .
the turning of Africa into a warren for the commercial hunting of
black-skins, signalised the rosy dawn of the era of capitalist production. These idyllic proceedings are the chief momenta of primitive
accumulation.

KARL MARX, *CAPITAL*

But our lives are accounted of no value, we are hunted after as the
prey in the desert, and doomed to destruction as the beasts that
perish.

OTTOBAH CUGOANO, *THOUGHTS AND SENTIMENTS ON THE
EVIL AND WICKED TRAFFIC OF THE SLAVERY*

IN 1440, the Portuguese navigator Antoine Gonzalez was sent
to the coasts of Guinea "to load his ship with seal-skins."[1] One
day when he had landed with ten of his men, he "discovered a
naked man who was carrying two spears and leading a camel; he
was a Moor who took fright and let himself be captured without
resisting."[2] On his way back to the ship, the captain found other
natives along the way, including a woman, whom he seized.
These two captives were probably "the first inhabitants of this
coast who fell into the hands of the Portuguese."[3] Encouraged
by this initial success, Gonzalez returned with more troops. "In
the obscurity of the night, he found other Moors. His men were

so close to these barbarians that they could grasp them in their arms without recognizing them by any mark other than their nakedness, and by the difference in their language; they killed three of them, took ten prisoners, and returned to their vessels."[4] In those years, the Portuguese ships returned to port bearing a new kind of merchandise. In their holds, alongside buffalo hides and a few "ostrich eggs," they brought back the first cargos of captive Africans. Back in Europe, they exhibited their trophies: "Everyone admired the color of the slaves," we read in the *Histoire générale des voyages.*[5]

The hunt for blacks had begun. It reached its full extent, however, only with the "discovery" of America and the rise of triangular trade—that is, with the establishment of Western capitalism.

In the early sixteenth century, Mvêmb'a a Ñzînga, the king of Manicongo, wrote a long letter to the king of Portugal, whom he still called his "brother." In it, he denounced what Portuguese slave-hunters were doing in his land: "The mentioned merchants are taking every day our natives, sons of the land and the sons of our noblemen and vassals and our relatives, because the thieves and men of bad conscience grab them wishing to have the things and wares of this Kingdom which they are ambitious of; they grab them and get them to be sold; and so great, Sir, is the corruption and licentiousness that our country is being completely depopulated."[6] His complaint was, of course, ignored. Despite African resistance, the slave trade grew.

The explorers' first raids and sporadic abductions gradually gave way to an organized system of supply. By means of force and by exploiting self-interest, the European powers were able to gain the collaboration of their African counterparts. Military alliances were forged in which weapons were traded for captives. These occasional agreements soon took the form of codified commercial partnerships. The slave trade had its rates, its depots, its rites, and its ceremonies. Demand grew, incessantly, and manhunting reached a paroxysm.

In the Congo, when the slave providers "no longer found on their own domains the merchandise that the Portuguese demanded of them," they extended their scope of action and made use of multiple forms of violence, ranging "from armed bands of increasingly numerous native accomplices that attacked a defenseless village or isolated family, to hunting, like birds of prey, individuals seeking food in the forest."[7] The European traders instilled among African peoples an incessant state of war which, as Kabolo Iko Kabwita explains, took the form less of "a classic war than that of manhunting."[8] In the province of Bembe de Benguela, the hunters used their own herds as bait and waited, hidden in the bush, until cattle thieves appeared, in order to capture them in turn.[9]

In addition to hunting in the strict sense, the techniques of acquiring slaves included enslavement for debts, penal servitude, and *poignage*, which the traveler Grandpré defined as "the action of seizing a man whom one sells, . . . a right that born princes exercise on any man who is not born their equal."[10] Once a potential prey was located, it was shown to a European "on some pretext, usually offering the victim a glass of brandy."[11] The trader could then judge the merchandise in the flesh. If he decided to buy it, "an agent approached the victim and leapt on him like a wild beast."[12]

The Europeans soon no longer found it necessary to practice this hunting themselves. Exploiting the relationships of domination internal to African societies, they delegated this task to local intermediaries. The division of labor between African suppliers and European buyers was seen as purely advantageous by the latter: it ensured regular supply and at the same time relieved them of the trouble of hunting. As in any policy of collaboration, the strategy consisted in corrupting—or, if necessary, subjugating—the leaders of the dominated peoples.

This delegation of the actual task of capturing was accompanied, in the discourse of the slave trade, by a transfer of responsibility. Here it was no longer necessary, as it had been in the case of the American Indians, to justify hunting natives. They were no longer hunted: they themselves did the hunting, so that if Africans were slaves, that was in reality their own doing. This was the imperialist argument regarding the "dark continent," according to which, as a nineteenth-century French missionary in Africa put it, "its primary tormentors are the Africans themselves."[13]

This argument, which was repeated, as we shall see, in several historical variations, is still in circulation today, but those who use it do not seem to realize that they are merely reappropriating one of the most worn-out motifs of the slave-trade discourse, which has been identified as such and regularly demolished by abolitionists ever since the eighteenth century.

In its historical-ethnographic variant, this argument consists in presenting slave-hunting as a local African tradition, of which the transatlantic slave trade is supposed to be merely an extension—while making the latter appear, if necessary, as a relative improvement in the fate of the captives.[14] As early as the eighteenth century, Benezet, in what remains one of the most powerful denunciations of slavery in the early modern period, emphasized on the contrary the radical discontinuity of these practices: it was in fact only "long after the Portuguese had made a practice of violently forcing the natives of Africa into slavery, that we read of the different Negroe nations making war upon each other, and selling their captives. . . . [T]he Europeans are the principal cause of these devastations."[15] Mirabeau

extended the question to the economic area: "Why seek the reason for these wars in the customs of the Africans, when reason
finds it in the ferocious industry of European greed? Is there
any lack of proofs of our eagerness to incite these detestable battles? . . . There are slave traders, how could there not be sellers?
How cruel does one have to be to hunt men or buy them on the
market?."[16] Mirabeau founded his critique on commercial logic
itself: given the—logical and not chronological—anteriority of
the market with respect to the capture, of demand with respect
to supply, it was in fact the commercial activity of European
companies that formed slave-hunting's center of gravity.

The fact that blacks were reduced to slavery, that they were
the universal prey of whites, was to be explained in still another
way. Why is the trade limited to blacks? An answer to this
question was found: "It is no doubt from the inferiority of the
black race that was born this immense trade in slaves, of which
Negroland has been the inexhaustible source."[17] An explanation
which, it was claimed, "refutes the opinion of those who have
attributed the misfortunes of the African race solely to European traders."[18] Here we find once again the classic thesis that
Africans are themselves responsible for their enslavement, but
this time it is reformulated in terms of the determinist logic of
a theory of races.

Of course, the truth lay elsewhere. As a general director of
the slave trade in Senegal acknowledged, "It was very populous,
the soil rich; and if the people were industrious, they might, of
their own produce, carry on a very advantageous trade with
strangers; there being but few things in which they could be ex-
celled; *but* [he adds] *it is to be hoped, the Europeans will never let
them into the secret*" (emphasis in the original).[19]

The racist ideology that actively ensured in its own way that
this "secret" was never divulged also strove to encrypt socio-

economic relationships in a racial code. In an epistemological shift that was ultimately quite absurd, the task of explaining the historical disaster that was taking place in the contact between the European capitalist mode of production and African societies was thus entrusted, starting at the end of the eighteenth century, to zoologists and specialists in natural history.

In the wake of Aristotle, for centuries people had been seeking a sign that would make it possible to recognize slaves by nature. Modern scientists finally found one, without expending much effort: "Moreover, nature has better served modern masters than it did ancient ones. Skin color is a sign that cannot be mistaken by anyone and that provides in most of the New World the infallible *criterium* whose absence Aristotle seems to regret."[20] The theory of races provided a pseudo-scientific basis for the ancient category of the slave by nature, in a context in which it was acknowledged that the question of the Africans' natural servitude belonged, as Julien Joseph Virey summed it up, "no less to zoology than to politics."[21]

The great theoretical invention of imperialist racism consisted in this zoologizing of social relationships. The relations among species became the privileged model for conceiving the relations among peoples. It was in these terms that the slave trade's predatory practices were explained—and at the same time justified. This model did not exclude a limited perfectibility for inferior races, but within the strict boundaries of the hierarchy of races: "Just as a lapdog can never be transformed into a hunting dog, a negro will never become a Plato or an Aristotle";[22] a nineteenth-century French naturalist dared to affirm.

This racial theory of African slavery made it possible to combine two theses: blacks themselves were intrinsically responsible for their enslavement, and at the same time, and for precisely that reason, *they could do nothing about it*. They were in a sense completely responsible because they were the endogenous cause, and simultaneously not responsible because this cause was their nature itself. This idea was also applicable, though in a different sense, to European nations: by perpetrating their crimes, they were only conforming to the predatory urge that marked the superiority of their race.

This paradoxical argument for Africans' irresponsible responsibility was given still more subtle formulations in the register of moral philosophy and politics.

Blaming the victim is the most classical and familiar practice of aggressors and tormentors: it's his fault. The victim has not been attacked, he has *made himself* be attacked. He has elicited the violence that has been inflicted on him. One might even say that the very fact that he lets himself be treated in this way—and it matters little whether he really had a choice—clearly demonstrates that in some sense he *deserved* it. Voltaire was saying nothing else when he wrote regarding the slave trade: "We are severely reproached for this kind of traffic, but the people who make a trade of selling their children are certainly more blamable than those who purchase them, and this traffic is only a proof of our superiority. He who voluntarily subjects himself to a master is designed by nature for a slave."[23] And he goes on: "If it can be said that some people deserve to be slaves, it is in the sense that we sometimes say that a miser deserves to be robbed."[24] The Aristotelian argument for the slave by nature was now reinterpreted in the framework of a theory of blame and responsibility: a slave by nature is someone who makes himself the agent of his own servitude. But Voltaire immediately added the following corrective: "Someone who takes advantage of another person's weakness or cowardice in order to reduce him to slavery is no less guilty. . . . [T]hese crimes are the work of the Europeans, who have inspired in the Blacks the desire to commit them, and who pay them for having committed them. The Blacks are only the accomplices and instruments of the Europeans; the latter are the real guilty ones."[25]

Beyond the apparent contradiction, the two theses actually played on two distinct concepts of culpability: a notion of moral responsibility and a notion of penal responsibility. Penally, the robber is the only guilty one, because it is he who actively commits the offense. However, the person who, by negligence or by vice, invites, as it were, the robbery, is still guilty in a certain sense, even if the act of the offense cannot be legally attributed to him. This is the idea of a behavior that leads others to commit a crime. If the victim of a robbery cannot be condemned, one can still continue to think privately that he nonetheless invited it. That is the idea that Voltaire wanted to instill in the reader's mind.

Even if they at first seem to be antinomic, these two assertions converge in fact toward the same basic thesis: whether they are made the agents of their own enslavement or the Europeans' passive auxiliaries, simple "tools" in their hands, in either case Africans are placed under the sign of a radical inferiority. First, they are recognized as active subjects, as agents, but in a paradoxical way, because this subjectivity is granted them provisionally only the better to make them the subjects of their own alienation. Their autonomy consists solely in the negation of their own autonomy, since it consists in selling themselves. But then this minimal power of action is itself denied: when they are seen as the Europeans' accomplices, Africans are revealed not to be agents, even of their own servitude: they are purely passive instruments of an alien will. It is the Europeans who make them do what they do. The inferiority posited in the first stage is not only not carried over into the second, but is accentuated to the point of denying them any power of action, even and including in the mode of collaboration. In short, on the pretext of recognizing European responsibility (how could it be denied?), the argument actually ends up affirming not the Africans' *innocence* but their irresponsibility—a fundamental irresponsibility that is connected with the substantial inferiority of an ethnic order. Africa becomes an absolute nonsubject.

This way of framing the problem of the responsibility for slavery leads to what might be called the *victim's dilemma*: either one recognizes that Africans have an autonomy of action (but then they have to be made the agents of their own alienation, their own tormentors), or one defines them as pure victims, simple objects for Europeans (but then we do so at the cost of negating their power of action). In the first case, they are considered to be co-responsible for the crimes of the slave trade; in the second case, they are recognized as victims, but thereby they are also seen as having no autonomous power of action and consequently as lacking any resource of their own for freeing themselves. This antinomy constitutes a powerful trap that ends up imprisoning in a complete political impasse those who fall into it.

The question, of course, is in what way blaming the oppressed is the necessary condition for granting that they have a political subjectivity. Here there is a confusion: whether slaves are recognized as responsible for their liberation, in the sense in which that task is for them to carry out, does not imply that they are responsible for their oppression, in the sense that they invited it. The idea that we have to impute to the oppressed the historical responsibility for their enslavement so that the task of emancipating them can be their own is a sophism.

But this problem, which the Enlightenment framed as a moral antinomy, was about to combine with another kind of thought. This change appeared clearly in the work of Hegel.

We recall the master/slave dialectic: if the slave is a slave, that is because he has preferred living in servitude to dying in order to defend his freedom. In a sense, therefore, he has chosen this condition; it "depends on the person's own will, whether he shall be a slave or not, just as it depends upon the will of a people whether or not it is to be in subjection. Hence slavery is a wrong not simply on the part of those who enslave or subjugate, but of the slaves and subjects themselves."[26] Because he has not chosen death, the slave has in fact accepted a form of voluntary servitude, in a kind of tacit pact between consciousnesses:[27] "There is always something of the order of right in the fact that another enslaves me. I could have died."[28]

Hegel's adoption of the thesis of the slave's responsibility has sometimes been presented as a paradoxically emancipatory gesture which, while affirming the tacit consent of the oppressed to their oppression, at the same time restored to them—and therein its emancipatory dimension is supposed to consist—the will that is otherwise denied them. In this reading, blaming the oppressed is thus interpreted as an injunction urging them to regain control over their own liberation. By thus placing the ball in the slaves' court, Hegel is supposed to have made their self-emancipation thinkable.[29]

The interpretation is tempting. But so far as Hegel's position is concerned, I think this reading is false. Other texts leave hardly any room for ambiguity: "Europeans have been blamed for having instigated slavery; but this is not true, because earlier slaves were eaten when they were captured in war; now, at least, they are sold to men. The Negro does not naturally exist as free; he is the contrary. Slavery being entirely illegitimate, for their sake slaves should be immediately granted their freedom; but the most terrible consequences ensue, as in the French colonies. Freedom has to be inculcated in Negroes by taming their nature."[30] In this claim that the intra-African slave trade began earlier and that the fate of the deported peoples was relatively improved by it,[31] which amounts to a defense of Europe by partially denying its historical responsibility, we find familiar elements. It is followed by the classic Hegelian thesis that freedom is not a natural determination (people are not born free; they have to become free). Except that here this thesis takes the form of a racist postulate according to which Negroes, bogged down in nature, are necessarily deprived of any consciousness of freedom. Finally—and this is crucial for the understanding of Hegel's position regarding the Haitian revolution, for it is to that event that he is referring when he mentions the "French colonies"—he rejects the option of immediately freeing the slaves because of the "terrible consequences," that is, the political violence that would be entailed by any armed insurrection against a system of domination as coercive as the slaveholding regime's.[32] To this scenario, which is none other than that of self-emancipation, Hegel opposes a paternalistic pedagogy of freedom, founded on the racist postulate of a nature of the "Negro race" that has to be tamed, that is, moderated by force. The project is that of a gradual abolition of slavery, conducted under the guidance of colonial authorities, in an orderly and disciplined manner.[33] Here we are very distant from the image of Hegel as a secret admirer of Toussaint Louverture.

Thus, instead of positing the thesis of African responsibility as the first, paradoxical stage in a process of self-emancipation, Hegel posits it as the starting point for a limitation of political action on the part of slaves. To self-emancipation he prefers, in a paternalistic schema, a scenario of gradual abolition. The political responsibility for their liberation eludes black slaves precisely in proportion to the ontological responsibility that is assigned to them in their servitude.

So we arrive at an impasse, because while Hegel makes the responsibility for slavery rest on the slaves themselves since they did not choose a fight to the death, he elsewhere denies them the political option of engaging in that fight when it presents itself in concrete form in the historical situation. This is a typical case of the self-contradictory injunction.

This is all the more problematic because Hegel, as we will see, not only refuses to allow black slaves the political option of fighting to the death, but still more radically denies that such a phenomenon could even *exist* for them.

On the one hand, he writes: "Those who remain slaves suffer no absolute injustice; for he who has not the courage to risk his life to win freedom, that man deserves to be a slave."[34] But on the other, when he encounters actual acts of courage, manifest acts of resistance in which Africans prefer, in the very terms of his own dialectic, freedom to a life in servitude, he reinterprets them in such a way as to deny them: "The distinguishing feature of the negroes' contempt for humanity is not so much their contempt for death as their lack of respect for life. . . . The great courage of the negroes, reinforced by their enormous physical strength, must also be ascribed to this lack of respect for life; for they allow themselves to be shot down in the thousands in their wars with the Europeans. . . . For in fact life is of no value if it does not have a worthy object."[35] Thus, when Africans engage in a fight to the death, it is not because they have attained a consciousness of freedom, transcending both the sensitive attachment to life and the fear of dying; if they die in combat, that is not a sign that they defy death but, on the contrary, a proof that they despise life. Here again Hegel's racist postulate is manifest: excluded from history, imprisoned in nature,[36] the Negro cannot have a consciousness of freedom, nor, consequently, the slightest notion of the value of human life. So that for him, the sacrifice of his life does not constitute a sacrifice. Negroes, Hegel says, "die heedlessly."[37] As a result, their seeming courage is not real courage, but pure unconsciousness. If Africans fall in large numbers in battles against Europeans, that is not for the very relevant reason that the latter have guns while the former do not: if they are massacred, that is because they *themselves* despise their own lives. In contrast, human life was, as we know, held in high regard by European traders raised on the milk of Christianity—with one reservation, however: only when the life concerned was their own.

In this fantastic inversion of reality, European massacres are attributed to the victims' contempt for *their own lives.* The proof? That the practice of slave-hunting is widespread in Africa: "This contempt or scant regard in which some humans are held by others, is also to be found among Negroes in the state of slavery, which is very widespread among them."[38] In a movement of reversal and projection with which we are by now familiar, the slaveholders' contempt for the lives of blacks is thus attributed to the Africans themselves. As Marx was wont to say about Hegel, everything is turned on its head. However, in the eighteenth century the slave Ottobah Cugoano had, in a way, responded to Hegel in advance. Who scorns life? For "the traders in Negroes," he wrote, "our lives are accounted of no value, we are hunted after as the prey in the desert, and doomed to destruction as the beasts that perish."[39]

If therefore Hegel makes slaves responsible for their enslavement because they have not been able to risk death, as soon as he sees Africans actually engaging in a battle to the death he denies it by reinterpreting it as insignificant. But what is the function of this self-contradictory injunction? Saying that the slave regime could not endure if slaves rejected it at the cost of their lives amounts to presupposing that *they do not reject it.* The effect consists in denying the reality of slave resistance. Under cover of escaping from paternalism by paradoxically assigning to the oppressed the subjective responsibility for their enslavement, the existence of another form of subjectivity that is actual and real is occulted: African slaves' massive, persistent desire for emancipation, to which an impressive mass of narratives and documents testifies from the very beginning of the slave trade.

If Africans are radically excluded from the Hegelian dialectic—and thus also from political subjectivity—that is first of all because of a racist postulate that deprives them of consciousness of life and liberty. But it is certainly also because the point of departure for the relationship of consciousness that is established in the experience of modern slavery does not correspond to the canonical schema of the Hegelian phenomenology of the master and the slave. The initial situation is in fact not a face-off between two undifferentiated consciousnesses that, through a free confrontation, will establish a relationship of domination, but instead a situation in which domination already exists and in which one party is already running away because the other is pursuing him. A different starting point that inaugurated, as we will see, a quite different dialectic.

CHAPTER 6

The Dialectic of the Hunter and the Hunted

Their masters take pleasure in hunting them like wild animals. . . .
[T]hey boast about having killed a brown Negro, as in Europe people
take pride in having killed from behind a fallow deer or a roe deer.
MARIE JEAN ANTOINE NICOLAS DE CARITAT, MARQUIS DE
CONDORCET, *RÉFLEXIONS SUR L'ESCLAVAGE DES NÈGRES*

I myself must be
The feast of those on whom I fed, the chase
Of that I hunted, and shall dearly pay
In bloody quittance for their death.
SOPHOCLES, *PHILOCTETES*

IN THE FIFTEENTH CENTURY, in his *Chronicle of Guinea*, Gomes
Eanes de Zurara tells of a raid the Portuguese made on a village
on the coasts of Africa: "Shouting 'Santiago! St. George! Portugal!' they fell on them and killed and captured as many as they
could. Then you might have seen mothers abandon their children and husbands abandon their wives, each trying to flee as
quickly as possible. Some of them drowned themselves in the
sea, while others sought refuge in their huts, and still others hid
their children under the coastal grasses, seeking in that way to
protect them from danger."[1]

FIGURE 3. Hunting a fugitive slave (1840). *The American Anti-Slavery Almanac for 1840*, p. 13.

To grasp the specific process involved in the experience of modern slavery, to describe the relationship of consciousnesses that was established in it, we have go back to the starting point: the moment of pursuit that precedes the capture.

The guiding question is how a political subjectivity can be constituted in a situation where one is a prey. How, in such a practical configuration, can one become a subject, and what kind of subject? How, being shaped by the hunting relationship, can a hunted consciousness transcend its status as prey and begin a movement of liberation?

Unlike in the Hegelian schema, the point of departure is not a face-to-face confrontation of two equal consciousnesses with interchangeable positions. Slaveholding domination does not arise from an open struggle but rather from a relationship, which is dissymmetrical from the outset, of manhunting. Here, even before operations begin, the hunter is already in a position to be the master. He knows his power and his material supremacy. The prey, taken by surprise, is not in a position to confront a group of hunters. At first, it has no choice but to flee.

The experience of hunting establishes for the prey a relationship to the world that is structured by a radical anxiety. Each perception, including that of its own body, becomes a foreboding of danger. Being constantly on the watch is what characterizes the animal,[2] and it is in this sense that being hunted animalizes humans. Olaudah Equiano, hidden in the forest, listening to the sounds of the night, "began to consider that, if possibly I could escape all other animals, I could not those of the human kind. . . . Thus was I like the hunted deer: 'Ev'ry leaf, and ev'ry whispering breath / Convey'd a foe, and ev'ry foe a death.' "[3]

The prey's experience is that of becoming an isolated individual, cut off from his fellows, each trying to save his own skin. Then the experience of capture makes him feel his absolute impotence—a scene internalized by each one, in panic, as proof of the master's omnipotence.

The pursuit and capture are followed by loading onto the slave ship. It is there that an initial form of the battle to the death can begin: "On leaving this area, we would have preferred death to life. We planned to burn the ship and all die together in the flames."[4] But here we are not in a situation in which, dialectically, the act of exposing oneself to death can make it possible, by winning the battle, to live free. Even if the mutiny succeeds, the ship, lost in the middle of the ocean, becomes a floating coffin. There is no escape. Revolt is a pure act of heroic resistance.

The only form of freedom that can be chosen at this point is freedom in death, that is, an abstract figure of liberation. The space of the slave ship, because it confined people to this tragic choice, was paradigmatic of the domination over slaves dreamed of by the masters: a space with no escape hatch.[5] This "choice" between freedom in death and life in servitude was part of the apparatus of domination—it was the sole kind of choice, an impossible choice—that slave power intended to leave its prey. The terms of this alternative—slavery or death—were the ones the masters wanted. Since for the slaves the only way to be free was to be dead, matters could proceed apace. So it is troubling to see philosophical thought adopting as its own this alternative, forgetting its origin and function and treating it as a speculative necessity rather than what it was, namely a practical dilemma forged by the masters in which the sole way to be free was to die, and in which even the fact of continuing to be alive could be interpreted as tacit assent to one's own servitude.

Being prepared to die for one's freedom is no doubt the necessary condition for engaging in an authentic battle for liberation, but the latter has no chance of succeeding so long as heroic suicide remains the only possible outcome. Applied without qualification to the situation of modern slaves, Hegel's requirement that they have contempt for death makes it possible to formulate only an abstract morality of freedom, not a strategy for liberation.

In this first stage, the fundamental structure of the servile consciousness, at least as the master wants it to be, is imprisoned in this nonchoice between existence as one of the living dead and an abstract liberation in death. The basic problem of slave rebellions was how to escape this nonchoice, how to move beyond the terms of this imposed alternative. The difficulty was to find forms of action that allowed slaves to prefer, not abstract freedom in death to death in "life" in slavery, but rather life itself to this living death that was made for them. How could they reject this life, which was already a negation of life, except by committing suicide? That was the fundamental question with which the project of a slave politics collided from the outset. Reconciling the struggle for freedom with that for one's own life was a difficult task, because everything in the system of domination tended to separate these two requirements, which are, however, inseparable.

Slaves themselves described "life" in servitude on the plantations as a nonlife, an existence as one of the living dead.[6] American films about zombies can be interpreted as a return of the slaveholding repressed. A master kills men whom he later reanimates in the form of dead bodies in order to make them act for his benefit.[7] But in doing so he endows them with a dangerous strength. As the female character in *Revenge of the Zombies*[8] repeats in a monotonous voice, just before she submerges the master in the shifting sands of a marsh, "You can't hurt me, you can't kill me, you can't control me." The film's motto is just as explicit: "Dead men can't die." By making the life of the slave a nonlife, the masters take the risk that slaves will no longer have anything to lose when they are confronted with the choice of a battle to the death. Deprived of the weapon of death, that "absolute master," the masters no longer have any authority. But this scenario also illustrates an impasse: the revolt of the zombies certainly triumphs over the master, but it can restore to the dominated only a phantasmatic freedom. Their condition of living death is irreversible. They are doomed, even if they do away with the oppressor, to perpetual mourning for their past life, their life before they were captured, their only true life. The sole form of freedom that they can obtain by means of this strange strength that they draw from the fact that they see themselves as already dead is still an abstract figure of freedom, a freedom of the living dead.

How can one move beyond such a living death? Orlando Patterson shows that doing so requires a double negation: "For the slave, freedom begins with the consciousness that real life

comes with the negation of his social death. . . . Freedom—life—
is a double negation; for his [the slave's] life is already a negation of life, and the reclamation of that life must therefore be
the negation of that negation."[9] And yet, he goes on, "freedom
is more than just a double negation. It is continuously active
and creative,"[10] and not merely a return to a form of freedom
anterior to the capture.

The former slave and black leader Frederick Douglass
recounted his fight with the "negro-breaker" Edward Covey:
"Mr. Covey seemed now to think he had me, and could do what
he pleased; but at this moment—from whence came the spirit
I don't know—I resolved to fight; and, suiting my action to the
resolution, I seized Covey hard by the throat; and as I did so, I
rose. He held on to me, and I to him. My resistance was so entirely unexpected that Covey seemed taken all aback. He trem-
bled like a leaf. This gave me assurance, and I held him uneasy,
causing the blood to run where I touched him with the ends of
my fingers." Douglass comments, "This battle with Mr. Covey
was the turning point in my career as a slave. It rekindled the
few expiring embers of freedom, and revived within me a sense
of my own manhood. It recalled the departed self-confidence,
and inspired me again with a determination to be free. The grat-
ification afforded by the triumph was a full compensation for
whatever else might follow, even death itself."[11] Paul Gilroy has
described this as "Douglass's transformation of Hegel's meta-
narrative of power into a meta-narrative of emancipation."[12]
Douglass puts at the end what in Hegel comes at the beginning: the moment of the battle to the death appears as what dis-
solves the relationship of domination and not what constitutes
it. This shift—a move that all revolutionary uses of Hegel's text
have repeated—leads to a reversal of the *Phenomenology*, turning it against itself in order to make it a theory of insurrection.

Whereas Hegel made labor and discipline the operators of an internal overcoming of domination—and as we have seen, in perfect correspondence with his political positions, which were those of a paternalistic abolitionism—slaves sometimes forced other paths to be taken.

In this new scenario, the sole possible outcome of the battle is no longer abstract freedom in death, whether in the form of suicide or a spectral liberty. Another possibility is opened up— one that belongs, paradoxically, to orthodox Hegelianism, despite the shift that it presupposes with regard to the original: that of a liberation in life through the mediation of a confrontation with the risk of dying.[13] But the dialectical movement still has to be able to operate: once life is put at stake in combat, the choice of fighting is actually converted into a choice of life only in the case in which the confrontation makes it possible, through victory, to actually reconcile the will to freedom with the desire for life. But this reconciliation is neither abstract nor automatic. It is a wager whose success depends on givens that are independent of the pure movement of consciousness: the situation, the propitious moment, the power relationship—in short, a whole strategic and political context.

Long before the direct battle took place, slaves had another, more immediate option: escape. Slaves in the French colonies had a word for it: escaping from one's master was called "stealing one's own corpse."[14] Freedom, impossible *here*, took on the aspect of an *elsewhere*. Liberation was conceived as a relationship to space rather than time, to geography rather than history.

Whereas from the beginning of the slave trade efforts were made to cast the blame for slavery on the slaves themselves, on the pretext of recognizing them as subjects, the massive fact of escapes allowed for an entirely different conception of slave subjectivity: "What blindness!" exclaims Schoelcher.

"The colonists are mad enough to maintain that the Negroes like slavery, and their sole concern is to prevent escapes and marronages!"[15]

When all precautions had failed, there remained no recourse except to track down the escapees. This was the hunt for "maroons"—a term that was generally applied to all "animals that have escaped Man's yoke"[16]; but especially to slaves who had fled their master's home.

A specialist was assigned to carry out this policing task. When a slave had escaped, the *ranchero*, a "manhunter attached as a guard to the household . . . whistled up his dogs, took his gun and his saber, and left for this strange hunt."[17] In Brazil, the occupation of slave-hunter was exercised by "a veritable paramilitary corporation—the *homens-do-mato* (woodsmen)—whose purpose was to track down fugitives and destroy the *quilombos*."[18] The slave-owners also resorted to a system of bounties, offering a reward for the capture of the fugitive, dead or alive. In the Antilles, bounty hunters "roamed the woods and mountains, carrying ropes to tie up the unfortunates whom they happened to take by surprise. . . . Their habit was to cut off the dead man's hand in order to take it to the government, which paid a bounty for this kind of offering."[19] In American newspapers, advertisements of rewards for "runaway slaves" sometimes included the following explanation: "Anyone at all is authorized to kill him and destroy him by whatever means are deemed suitable, without fear of being prosecuted in any way."[20] Fugitive slaves, who could be killed with impunity, thus took the place of wolfmen in ancient law, but in the framework of a different juridical rationality: they were chattels, objects of ownership, and as such could be killed at the command of their legitimate owner.

One of the most twisted procedures of slave power consisted in delegating the hunt for fugitive slaves to their former companions in misfortune.[21] This was done, as a French deputy to the National Assembly explained in 1792, because "people of color are far more skilled than whites in hunting down fugitive blacks in the mountains, and for that reason nothing equals the fear that they inspire in the slaves."[22] Dividing, hunting, terrorizing, those were the principles of a good colonial government, and in order to implement them, one had to be able to win over suitable auxiliaries within the dominated group. One of the great tactics of slave power consisted in making a place, by turning it against itself, for the powerful desire for recognition that slaves continued to feel. In the manipulation of this desire, the slave-masters had at their disposal a force that was "more powerful than any whip."[23] They responded to aspirations to escape servitude by channeling them into a sort of promotion internal to the slave system: you will no longer be our slaves, but rather our huntsmen.

This recourse to auxiliaries also spared masters the trouble of doing the hunting themselves. They supervised the hunt; they participated in it at a distance, like a lord at a foxhunt, but without having to descend to the level of their prey. The problem, in fact, is that hunting presupposes a form of empathy with the prey: to track prey effectively, one has to put oneself in its place. But this mental operation implied a denial of the absolute social distance between masters and their slaves that the hunting relationship sought precisely to reinstate. Thus, blacks were used against other blacks, on the racist assumption that the latter understood their "kind" better, but also in order to avoid having to *tangle with them*. It was a hunt, not a fight among equals. A third term had to be brought in to mediate.

Dogs also played this role. In the Caribbean islands, "black-eating dogs" or "bloodhounds" were specially trained for hunting fugitive slaves. After the young dogs had undergone lengthy

FIGURE 4. Training a dog for hunting maroons in Santo Domingo. "The Mode of Training Blood Hounds in St. Domingo, and of Exercising Them by Chasseurs," in Marcus Rainsford, *An Historical Account of the Black Empire of Hayti* (London: Albion, 1805), p. 422.

training using black-painted dummies filled with meat and dripping with blood, "they were tried out on living men by taking them, along with a well-trained pack, on a hunt for fugitive Negroes."[24] In the middle of the nineteenth century, announcements like this one could still be found in American periodicals: "Dogs for Negroes. The undersigned, having bought the whole pack of hunting hounds for Negroes, trackers for such, offers himself for hire in hunting down and capturing fugitive Negroes. His prices are three dollars a day for the hunt, and fifteen dollars for the capture of the fugitive."[25]

Whereas in the master-slave dialectic the relationship of consciousnesses had a fundamentally dual structure, in the hunting situation the master almost never confronts his prey directly. He uses intermediaries, mercenary hunters or hunting dogs. This is a schema with three terms rather than two.

Because of this mediation and the imbalance of the forces involved, the master never feels, when he launches a manhunt, that he is putting his own life at stake. On the contrary, everything is done to ensure that his life is never threatened. To be sure, in a few rare cases he might be killed, but that is an accident, not a structuring given of the relationship.

Thus we obtain that other deviation from the schema of the *Phenomenology*: the master's consciousness is not that of the one who has proven himself able to face death, but rather that of the one who has the power to put others' lives at risk without ever having to risk his own. If the master is recognized as an autonomous self-consciousness, that is precisely because he *does not have to* expose himself to death. In order to be the master, he has not risked his life, he has not scorned life in himself as he does in others, but *only* in others. His consciousness as a dominator is manifested in this exclusive play with others' lives: it is in the eyes of the prey caught by dogs that he sees that he is the master, because what he sees is that for the prey, he is death, that is, the absolute master.

Thus, contrary to the epic legend of the masters, their power does not derive from a victory won at the end of a free confrontation of consciousnesses. The genealogy of modern slavery is not that of a duel but that of a hunt.

The joys of manhunting occupy a particular place in the history of the dominators' affects—an experience that mixes in a complex way cruelty, pleasure, and the feeling of power. For masters as well, hunting fugitives became a kind of aristocratic game:

> In the colonies, people often indulged in the pleasure of forming hunting parties to catch fugitive blacks, with as much eagerness and publicity as one might in Europe put into hunting boars, or any other wild beast. . . . I knew a lady in a colony who had often engaged in this amusement, to which she invited her lady friends. When the unfortunate fugitive, caught by the dogs, wounded and brought to bay, begged for the compassion and mercy of those who were hunting him, they laughed at his sufferings, insulted his misfortune: then they cut off his head and took it to the local administrative center in order to get the bounty.[26]

The former slave William Craft describes the same kind of phenomenon in North America: "The greatest excitement prevails at a slave-hunt. The slaveholders and their hired ruffians appear to take more pleasure in this inhuman pursuit than English sportsmen do in chasing a fox or a stag."[27]

To the mediated pleasure of war—mediated in that it implies overcoming the fear of combat and death—Norbert Elias opposed the immediate pleasure of manhunting.[28] Hunting is defined not as a battle to the death but as an execution temporally delayed: "It was the dogs that killed, whereas the main and essential amusement of the exercise lay in fact solely in the pursuit. . . . It was the tension of the simulacrum of combat itself and the pleasure that it gave the human participants that was predominant. Killing foxes was easy. All the rules of hunting were conceived to increase the difficulty, to prolong the competition, to delay the victory . . . because the excitement of the hunt itself had become the main source of enjoyment."[29]

The hunter scorns prey that are too easy to take. This has to do with a dialectic of desire. It is the freedom of the adverse consciousness that is desired, in the mode of its negation. But the freer the object, the more intense the pleasure taken in this negation. That is why "of all the known forms of hunting, manhunting is certainly the one that is the most exciting. It has the superiority of being a battle between two intelligences of the same nature."[30]

But even though all its value is based on this shared nature, manhunting is paradoxical in that it dehumanizes those who engage in it, and not only the prey: "A few paces away, I discerned, immobile and lying on his belly, a young soldier who was usually of a gentle and inoffensive nature. His humor, related to his physical appearance, would have found shedding a sheep's blood repugnant. But manhunting had transfigured him. His head covered by leaves, his chin resting on the earth, he had crept there on his hands and knees, and his eyes persistently fixed on a single point in the marsh, he was lying in wait, like a flesh-eating animal, for an invisible prey."[31] If the human prey is animalized, so is the hunter, insofar as he has very animal-like feelings. Those who take pleasure in the cruel joys of manhunting are transformed and become savage. In the colonial context, this is the critical theme favored by Aimé Césaire, the transformation of the masters into beasts or savages: "Colonization works to decivilize the colonizer, to brutalize him in the true sense of the word, to degrade him, to awaken him to buried instincts."[32]

For the fugitive slave, the experience of being hunted produces different effects on his consciousness. By escaping, he has certainly regained his freedom of movement, but he knows that he is still being pursued. His new life is a tracked existence. This still amounts, at a certain distance, to a specific form of subjection. The prey is the *object* of a hunt. To arrive at his full freedom, he has to recover his subjectivity from this position of an object. But how is such a reversal possible?

In his *Critique de la raison dialectique*, Sartre explains that "an individual who is hunted, who is tracked down in the practical field by a group organized for a man-hunt . . . cannot attempt to break out of the circle unless he manages to reinteriorize his objectivity for the group, that is to say, to decipher his own acts in terms of the common freedom of his enemies: the action I am about to perform is precisely what they expect of the object that I am for them."[33]

In order to anticipate the reactions of his pursuers, the hunted man has to learn to interpret his own actions from the point of view of his predator. This internalization of the perspective of the other makes him develop an extreme prudence that at first takes the form of a paralyzing anxiety of a paranoid type: seeing himself in the third person, considering, with respect to each of his acts, how they might be used against him.

But this anxiety can later be transformed into reasoning. The hunt mobilizes, in fact, a certain form of thought: a mental attitude that, on the basis of the desire for an object, makes a man think, as Hobbes explains, "upon the next means of attaining it, and that again of the next, etc. . . . And this the Latins call *Sagacitas*, and we may call *Hunting* or *Tracing*; as dogs trace beasts by the smell, and men hunt them by their footsteps; or as men hunt after riches, place, or knowledge."[34] The problem with the prey is that he leaves traces that make it possible to track him down. Flight, the means of escape, also becomes, in a tragic circle, a way of being found. But the fugitive can foresee the sagacity of his pursuers and cover his tracks. The art of escape is a semiotic art, an art of mastering the traces. In his flight, the American slave Henry Bibb met, coming toward him on the road, a group of white men on horseback. They passed by him without showing any sign of interest, but the fugitive interpreted this indifference as a ruse, and suspected them of having in reality gone to get hunting dogs at a nearby farm. Thus, they would return to the place where they had met him and unleash the dogs along the wayside to find his trail: "I thought my chance of escape would be better, if I went back to the same side of the road that they first went, for the purpose of deceiving them; as I supposed that they would not suspect my going in the same direction that they went, for the purpose of escaping from them."[35] Retracing one's steps and turning aside to trick the pack is called, in the vocabulary of hunting, *faire hourvari*: "The stag, the roe deer, or the hare, etc. has performed a *hourvari* when, to confuse the dogs and cause them to lose the scent, it turns back in the direction from which it has come."[36] This stratagem involves what Sartre called a "dialogue in the sense of a rational antagonism" between the hunted man and his pursuers, since the action includes in its formulation as a strategic project the probable reactions of the adverse will that it seeks to counter.

In so doing, the prey escapes the state of simple objectification that constituted his point of departure. By including in his plan of action the logic of his predator, he envelops and internalizes it. Thus he acquires, at the end of this first dialectic of tracking, the mental abilities of a hunter, whereas he is still only a prey. If this new strategic aptitude does not yet allow him, at this stage, to frustrate his pursuers' intentions, it soon makes him capable of something quite different. The art of effective flight, insofar as it presupposes an intellectual mastery of cynegetic logic, paves the way for a reversal of the hunting relationship. The prey may cease to be an object tracked and transform himself into a subject, that is, initially, a hunter in turn.

In 1833, the authorities of the Île Bourbon (now Réunion) set a price on the head of a maroon named Charles Panon. They did so in vain. Several weeks later, a police officer who was taking a convoy of maroons to prison was attacked on the road: "It was in this battle that this officer, having been caught by his genitals, was soon overthrown and had only time to call for help by crying that he was being killed. . . . Charles Panon, whose audacity increases every day, seems to be the main perpetrator of this crime."[37] Anyone who tracks men like wild animals can expect to be bitten by them.

But slave escapes could also gain in intensity and take on a still more threatening and political dimension. The *quilombos* in which maroons gathered sometimes served as rear bases for guerilla activities.

In the Antilles, armed expeditions were launched against groups of fugitive slaves who had taken refuge in the woods, centers of potential insurrection that threatened colonial domination. Significantly, these military operations continued to be organized and to be conceived in terms of hunting. When the maroons of Trelawney revolted in Jamaica in 1796, the colonial Assembly resolved to bring from Cuba packs of dogs specially trained for hunting down fugitive slaves. Anticipating the "calumnies" that would certainly be formulated in the home country once the news of this decision became known, the planters sought justifications in moral philosophy and in the history of war, with, as Humboldt put it, "the full panoply of philosophical erudition."[38] Thus they emphasized that "Asiatics of all ages have used elephants in war,"[39] and that if the use of animals contravened the laws of war, the use of cavalry would no doubt also have to be prohibited. In any case, they were at war against a dangerous enemy, and the security of the whites justified everything. Relying on these arguments, on 15 December 1796, the authorities brought in from Cuba a troop of "Spanish hunters, almost all men of color, and a pack of a hundred dogs."[40] The recourse to dogs was explained by the tactical requirements of a guerilla war conducted against an elusive enemy, finding whose trace was the chief problem. But this was not all; it was also a matter of mental categories. Resorting to bloodhounds was a powerful psychological way of renewing and reimposing the absolute ontological gap between the masters and their slaves, which the insurrection had imperiled.

In this form of guerilla warfare carried on by the dominant against the dominated, the use of dogs expressed still another denial of the situation of combat. Treating civil war as a man-hunting operation amounted to continuing to deny the actual event, refusing to recognize the fact that the dominated had succeeded in imposing a situation of antagonism in which the possibility of a reversal of the power relationship was glimpsed, and no longer an ordinary disturbance of public order. In this kind of situation, manhunting becomes a means of waging _cynegetic war_—a kind of war that has the following characteristics: (1) it does not take the form of a direct confrontation, but of a process of tracking down; (2) the power relationship is marked by a radical dissymmetry in weapons; (3) its structure is not that of a duel: a third term is mobilized as a mediation; (4) the enemy is not recognized as such, that is, as an equal—he is only a prey; (5) use is made of nonnoble means related to policing or hunting rather than to the classical military register. Note that this travesty of civil war as a hunting operation leads inevitably to a burlesque effect which, in a macabre way, becomes the characteristic trait of all narratives of cynegetic war. _Cynegetic burlesque_ arises from the contrast between the baseness of the means employed and the grandeur of the style with which they are adorned. A sign of the times: the sole heroic motifs that the colonists still seemed to have at their disposal to ornament their narratives were the high deeds performed by their dogs.[41]

During the revolt in Santo Domino in 1802, the French army resorted to the same expedient as the citizens of Jamaica, but with a quite different outcome. In order to repress the maroons' insurrection, the authorities bought in from Cuba several hundred Spanish bloodhounds that had been "trained for hunting Negroes and Indians. . . . M. de Noailles, who had brought back these ferocious animals, was made their commander in chief; thus he became the *general of the dogs*."[42] In a letter announcing the arrival in the territory of twenty-eight bulldogs, Rochambeau, Napoleon's general, wrote, to explain the fact that no expenditure for feeding them had been included in the budget: "You have to give them Negroes to eat. I send you my warmest greetings. Signed: Rochambeau."[43] The operations began, but the maroons put up unexpected resistance. Forced to take refuge at Cap-Haitien, the French troops were cut off from their food supplies: "The last resource for the besieged troops was the fighting dogs that they had fed on the flesh of Negroes. The manhunters were obliged to eat their packs of dogs."[44]

What is peculiar to manhunting, what constitutes its danger but also its supreme aristocratic attraction, is the constant possibility of a reversal of the relationship: the prey might become a predator, the hunted a hunter. Manhunting is characterized by this fundamental instability: when the prey, refusing to continue to be a prey and ceasing to run away, retaliates and tracks in turn, hunting becomes combat or a struggle. What is specific to the relation between hunting and predation, applied to humans by humans, is that the prey can learn, that it is obviously not a prey by nature, and that—as the masters may learn by bitter experience—the dominated can develop kinds of knowledge that are not the privilege of the masters: they can become hunters or strategists in their turn.

This reversal of positions is moreover the classical motif of all the narratives, the spring that underlies the scenarios of all the films about manhunts: the prey becomes a hunter and the hunter becomes the prey. That is why manhunting is "the most dangerous game," to borrow the title of a 1932 film by Irving Pichel.[45] Past and present manhunters would no doubt do well to meditate on this lesson to which all the narratives, both ancient and modern, attest: the hunter will be hunted, his weapon taken away and held at the other extremity by his former prey, who might smile slightly at the moment that he strikes the fatal blow. Before leaving the stage in a final explosion, the former hunters, defeated, may have time to ask this last question: "Why are you doing this?" And the former prey will answer, like the character played by Jean-Claude Van Damme in John Woo's *Hard Target* (1993): "Poor people get bored too."

Diderot, who rightly saw in the grouping together of maroons in liberated areas the seeds of a future revolution, had prophesied the advent of a black hero who would finally make a slave rebellion succeed: "Where is this new Spartacus, who will not find a Crassus? Then will the black code be no more; and the white code will be a dreadful one; if the conqueror only regards the right of reprisals!"[46] Thus we find immediately posed, along with the explicit prospect of a slave rebellion, the problem of political vengeance and revolution.

In the right of reprisal, the violence of the other provides the basis for the legitimacy of my reactive violence, but it is also this violence that determines my violence, its measure, its norm, and finally its form. Vengeance is mimetic. It imposes a system of heteronomy of action. Through a kind of tragic trick, it tends, at the same time that it is satisfied, to take revenge as well on the person who abandons himself to it, by making him become, in spite of himself, the exact reflection of the opponent he is fighting.

This is the fundamental problem of the dialectic of the hunter and the hunted as a political dialectic: how can one avoid remaining caught in the simple inversion of the relationship of predation, and instead move beyond hunting itself? The danger is, of course, that in order to win, the former prey will end up becoming the opponent from whom he wanted to escape.

Here too fiction has extensively staged this impasse of the dialectic of the hunter and the hunted. The film *Deadly Prey*[47] probably provides the most obvious illustration of this circularity. In a classic scene, the former prey tears off his pursuer's arm and strikes him with this member detached from his body. The hunted ends up the winner, but at the price of being transformed into a predator. In the final scene, after having made his former pursuer disrobe, he orders him with a bestial cry: "Run!"

This kind of nondialectical reversal, in which only the assignment of roles and not the structure of their relationship changes, has long been recognized as a danger by revolutionary political thought. The fact that revolutions have been able to take the form of vast manhunts that repeat, first against their adversaries and then against their own supporters, the relationships of predation against which they rose up, is no doubt the ultimate revenge of cynegetic power.

For the theoreticians of social revolution, coping with this danger implied radically extracting the question of political violence from the logic of vengeance. This was already summed up by Bakunin, correctly: "Political carnage has never killed parties; above all they have shown themselves to be completely powerless against the privileged classes, whose power resides much less in the men than in the positions provided for privileged men by the organization of things."[48] Political violence properly understood is not aimed at individuals, but at the positions that make them what they are. It is not a matter of *inverting* the relationships of predation, but of *abolishing* them.

Thus was posed, indirectly, the problem of the relationship to the state. Since the dawn of the modern period, the state had provided itself with a new, centralized apparatus for tracking and capture. In the Old World, one event in particular had allowed this hunting branch of the state to develop in a completely unprecedented way.

CHAPTER 7

Hunting the Poor

What! have you never, since you were first formed into a political
body, found out the secret of obliging the rich to make the poor
work? Are you still ignorant of the first principles of civil policy?
VOLTAIRE, *LES EMBELLISSEMENTS DE LA VILLE DE
CACHEMIRE*

The poor were hunted down. They were tracked and rounded up by
all police means, even by the fear of infamous tortures.
JULES MICHELET, *L'HISTOIRE DE FRANCE*

THE FOUNDING ACT OF POLICE HUNTING, the inaugural scene of
the roundup power that was to become that of modern policing,
is the immense hunt for the poor, idle people, and vagabonds
that was launched in Europe in the seventeenth century—first
with the Poor Laws of Elizabethan England, and then in 1656
in France, with the creation of the General Hospital, where "the
poor were to be interned and fed." In doing so, royal power
chose to solve the problem of poverty by the massive incarcera-
tion of the poor. Of course, in order to intern them, they had
first to be captured.

Posters were put up in the streets of Paris: begging was
prohibited in the city, on pain of being whipped, and later the
penalty was galleys for men and banishment for women. Agents

were sent to cruise the streets and seize any indigent people they found there. These special officers engaged by the General Hospital were assigned to "hunt down beggars."[1]

"Hunting" the poor was, of course, not a new practice. In Nevers, in 1572, "the great number of poor outsiders who had spread in the city . . . giving reason to fear either plague or a surprise attack, it was decided . . . to hire three or four men to look for them and drive them out."[2] At the end of the sixteenth century, in order to cope with the influx of poverty-stricken people, "guards are posted at the gates to prevent the poor, beggars, and vagabonds from entering the city, special officers are designated to pursue through the streets and arrest those who ask for alms; they are called 'beggar-hunters' or 'rascal-hunters.' "[3]

The guards posted at the entrance to the city were assigned to identify vagabonds and the homeless poor. They separated the desirables from undesirables on the basis of their faces, physiognomy, and clothes: "When a priest or pilgrim comes to the gates of the city, these gatekeepers may allow them to enter if their clothes and faces do not make them suspect of being beggars."[4] They selected and excluded, but they did not intern.

The beggar-hunters, on the other hand, "hunted inside the city."[5] They patrolled, identified suspects, and arrested and expelled them.[6] Even the Church had its hunters of the poor. There was the "beggar-hunter of the cathedral," whom Furetière defined as "the Swiss or beadle who drives poor beggars and dogs away from the churches,"[7] and who served chiefly to disperse crowds of beggars on days when mass was celebrated.

In Switzerland, voyagers could long encounter on the roads of the canton of Bern "beggar-hunters . . . armed with an unusually long rapier and wearing an enormous three-cornered hat with a voluminous plume." But we are told that they "nonetheless do not intimidate the indigent, whom they are supposed to frighten."[8]

If these figures were familiar at the beginning of the modern period, their function up to that point had been only to disperse or expel. Hunting the poor meant *driving them out of the place where they were.* But with the new logic that instituted *le grand renfermement,* "the great confinement," the very meaning of *hunting* the poor changed. The poor were no longer sent back to the fields and forests, but captured in order to be confined within the walls of the General Hospital. According to Foucault, this was "the first time that the purely negative measures of exclusion had been replaced by the idea of confinement: the unemployed were no longer simply expelled or hunted down, and responsibility was taken for them by the nation, but at the expense of their individual liberty."[9] The function of a modern police force conceived as an instrument of capture and internment arose in this event.

It would be a mistake, however, to think that by a regulated process of succession hunting-expelling was entirely replaced by hunting-confining. In reality, these two forms of exclusion coexisted, but they were distributed differentially depending on the status of the subject concerned. In seventeenth-century Dijon, the city's rascal-hunters were given different instructions depending on whether they were dealing with a local beggar or a poor "foreigner."[10] "If they encounter some poor person from the city itself who is begging, they are to take him to the hospital, pending arrangements made by the superintendents of the poor to punish him, if it so befalls; and if he is a foreigner, he is taken back outside the gates."[11] Intern the locals, expel the strangers: those were the two fundamental modalities of exclusion. But the foreigners among the foreigners, the undesirables among the undesirables were the Bohemians. If the "hospital" functioned in general as an "apprenticeship and preface to the galleys . . . there was a class of men for whom this preface did not exist and who, de jure summarily, and without trial, were arrested and chained up. These were the Bohemians, also known as Egyptians. They were hunted, tracked down, captured like wild animals; the women's heads were shaved, then they were whipped, branded, and expelled from the kingdom; the men were chained to the rowing bench in a galley for life."[12] André Zysberg tells how these "nomads who had galley physiognomies" were treated. Some of them were judged by the provost-marshals with a remarkable iniquity and dishonesty, while others were immediately put in chains without trial. The intendants, like Pellot in Tours or Foucault in Montauban, engaged in hunting the poor: "I cause to be tracked down," one of them wrote, "all the Bohemians and vagabonds in my department . . . that would be the way to purge the province of all homeless people and provide good convicts for the king's galleys."[13]

The practice of hunting the poor continued in the eighteenth century: "The same scenes and still more horrible ones, after the edict of 1724. . . . Immense roundups brought into the hospitals great numbers of beggars and vagabonds. . . . They were crowded, pell-mell, into the old cramped and foul hospices. 'Let them lie on straw and give them bread and water; they will take up less space,' were the instructions addressed to the superintendents by the controller general Dodun."[14] By the end of the century of the Enlightenment, the practice had been institutionalized all over Europe: "The number of police officers has been increased in Denmark to ensure that beggars are arrested. To that end, in Mecklenburg-Schwerin a law has created a corps of hussars. In most of the states of Germany, a numerous police force on foot and on horseback is customarily employed in hunting down beggars."[15]

But this policy of hunting the poor was not accepted without opposition. It implied that begging was a crime, even if, in the main line of medieval tradition, the beggar was still very widely considered a man of God. Thus, as Emmanuel Le Roy Ladurie explains, "hired agents, gatekeepers, rascal-hunters, and provost-marshals, all symbols of bourgeois order, tried in vain to incarcerate them. All those who participated in the old system of thought, who still believed, as people did in the Middle Ages, that begging was a sign of election—little people, lackeys, servants, children, nuns, tavern-keepers, and prostitutes—protected them, snatched them from the claws of the hunters of the poor, hid them in their homes, and then set them free."[16]

Despite royal decrees, the people continued to give alms to "their" poor and protect them. It was not rare that poor-hunters trying to seize a wretch were chased down and whipped by the people. Official reports lamented "the difficulty of arresting beggars connected with the people's animosity against the hospital's officers."[17] It was still more worrisome when attempts to arrest beggars sometimes led to riots. In 1659, just after the creation of the General Hospital, there were "eight seditions in Paris, with weapons, against the hospital's officers." In Montpellier, where "guards and poor-hunters were not popular and were often abused by the crowd," the council decided to "to give the poor-hunters of this city helmets with a badge bearing the city's coat of arms, in order to prevent them from being ill-treated in future."[18] Useless protections that stopped neither insults nor blows. It is said that the poor-hunters, weary and ill-paid, ended up leaving the poor alone in exchange for a little money.

However that may be, the system of capturing and interning ran up against an internal limit. The problem was simple, and a nineteenth-century author formulated it clearly: "How can all the beggars arrested be housed in the prisons? In a single year there were as many as fifty thousand of them."[19]

The notion was that the way to get rid of poverty was to intern the poor. As might have been expected, neither hunting the poor nor prohibiting begging made poverty disappear. They could not. And that probably did not matter, since the function of these measures lay elsewhere. As Michelet diagnosed it, "the court, the powerful, do not like to see these great troops of poor wretches wandering about, a living accusation of the administration." Then as now, if poverty could not be eradicated, the poor had to be made invisible. Moving from the embarrassing visibility of itinerant mendicancy to the tranquil invisibility of poverty interned—that was the chief function of hunting the poor to confine them.

But if internment was first of all a strategy for making poverty socially invisible, it was seen to have other virtues, and other uses were found for it. Once the poor were confined, they could finally be put to work. Enclosed within four walls, they could now be weaned from their "idle life," if necessary by beating them with gun-butts or sticks—or worse.

In England, the Poor Laws made charity a legal duty, imposing in turn forced labor, on pain of the most terrible punishments. In this punitive logic, "rebellious beggars were made to expiate their idleness by being thrown in prison."[20] Helping and punishing: the state's charity emerges against the background of this fundamental ambiguity.

The charitable state is also a hunting state, and behind its display of coercive benevolence we can discern a vague joy. This secret affinity linking charity and manhunting was revealed in novels, in a form that was still gentle:

"I had an amusement to propose to you."

"An amusement? What?"

"A hunt. . . . [O]nly, I never kill the game that I track, and sometimes . . . I help it live; it is a hunt for the poor that I wanted to
propose to you."

In a spontaneous movement quicker than thought, Camilla's
hand sought the young man's and pressed it.

"Oh!" she said in a vibrant voice, her eyes glistening, "that is an
amusement I certainly would not refuse."[21]

The blessed joy of charity relieves the rich man's troubled
conscience, and he finds comfort in the gratitude of the poor
person he has helped. But was this joy as pure as all that? In
another novel, an aristocrat confesses, "In this world, I love only
charity . . . but I am afraid, nonetheless, that I am not fundamentally good. . . . I take too much pleasure in hunting down
the poor."[22] This suspect pleasure did not disappear with the
rise of the legal form of charity constituted by public assistance.
Beneath state charity a cynegetic and penal logic could still be
discerned, which the proponents of religious charity, who thus
saw themselves deprived of the care of their poor, did not fail
to denounce: "We see armed men hunting down the indigent,
seizing them everywhere, and taking them by force to depots;
workshops are organized in which they are forced to labor, a penal code is developed for them in which laziness and inaptitude
are classified as crimes and punished as such—Thus laziness is
a crime, but only for the poor. The rich man can be lazy; justice
has two scales."[23]

What was actually going on in forced labor for the poor
was the physical and moral training of what was to become the
class of wage-earners. This vast operation of hunting the poor
in reality signed the birth certificate of the modern proletariat.

As Foucault explains, "Confinement, the signs of which are to be found massively across Europe throughout the seventeenth century, was a 'police' matter. In the classical age the word had a meaning that was quite precise, referring to a bundle of measures that made work possible and necessary to all those who could not possibly live without it."[24] Police power emerges as a class instrument, as the principal means of putting the dispossessed to work, of training them and inserting them by force into what was to become the market of wage labor.

But another idea appears as well. It is not only that the poor, because of their existence outside work, live a blameworthy life, but also that poverty forms at once the crucible and the shelter of crime. On 2 August 1764, Count Saint Florentin urged the intendant of Paris to "hunt down beggars and vagabonds, among whom thieves and even murderers are trained or take refuge."[25] With such formulations appears a new argument: if poor people have to be driven out, that is because they are potentially criminal. The logic was unanswerable: poverty was a crime, and if crime was to be eradicated, then the poor had to be hunted down.

The poor thus became a dangerous category. In the nineteenth century, the Paris police published communiqués like this one: "M. the Prefect of Police attaches the greatest importance to purging Paris of this population of mendicants, pimps, and criminals of all kinds who are constantly threatening our security and may constitute a genuine danger in certain political circumstances. Consequently, yesterday and today M. the Prefect of Police has had his agents carry out hunts in Paris. . . . He has had an exceptional number of vagabonds arrested. . . . Last night, the peace officer of the Halles brigade carried out another roundup of twenty-five vagabonds and homeless people."[26]

A medical vocabulary of purging excrements, the theme of insecurity, reference to the political threat posed by the dangerous classes, the practice of roundups formulated in the language of manhunts: in this short text we have almost all the elements of police hunting. The republican journalist Yves Guyot, who pointed out the complete absence of a legal framework for such arrests without a warrant, commented indignantly: "They call that purging. . . . Flushing out! rounding up! ordinary terms used to designate hunting the poor. The planters would not have spoken differently about hunting negro maroons."[27]

But the fact that extralegal aspect of these practices of capturing and interning could become a scandal testifies above all to a change in the status of police activity. For a long time, as Foucault explains, "hunting down of vagrants, beggars, and the idle; this practice of police selection, exclusion and imprisonment remained outside the field of the judicial, legal practice. . . . And then, at the beginning of the 19th century, the police enforcement of social selection was reintegrated into the judicial practice because, in the Napoleonic State, police, justice and penitential institutions were linked to each other."[28]

In this new context, the police was henceforth to be an arm of the judicial system, the penal power's apparatus for capturing.

CHAPTER 8

Police Hunts

> What next! You are stumpy, ugly, a toper. And it is said that you are a police agent into the bargain; she, on the other hand, is as handsome as the huntress Diana.
>
> HONORÉ DE BALZAC, *LE DÉPUTÉ D'ARCIS*

> The profession of the police officer seems to me the most amusing form, the supreme expression, of hunting: isn't it a manhunt? Since I am a serious hunter, you will understand my interest in it. I know no greater pleasure than that of riding across the steppe in pursuit of hares and foxes with a pack of greyhounds. But how much more wonderful it must be, more exciting, to track down men, to restart them, to drive them into the net! Let me participate in this diabolical pleasure that you enjoy.
>
> LEOPOLD VON SACHER-MASOCH, *LA PÊCHEUSE D'ÂMES*

IN 1907, an international competition for police dogs was held in Rouen. The police dog was then a recent invention. First used in Belgium and then in Germany, it was publicly presented in France on this occasion:

> This city's central police commissioner, complaining about the growing number of dangerous vagabonds to his German and Swiss colleagues who had gathered to participate in this competition, . . . the foreign police officers proposed an experiment. They organized a hunt under the direction of the French magistrate to which they brought their champion dogs. In a short time the vagabonds,

FIGURE 5. The battle between crime and devotion. "The murderous bandit, that man who is a wolf for man, and the dog, that friend of humanity, that guardian of society, are engaged in a battle. But don't worry, human vice will be punished and canine virtue will triumph." Paul Villers, "Le chien, gardien de la société," *Je sais tout*, no. 33 (15 October 1907): 361–368, esp. 365.

terrified and screaming, were flushed out of their hiding places, but those who fled were immediately caught by the implacable dogs and soon an enormous group of them was taken to police headquarters, the good dogs performing their natural task of shepherding.[1]

Such were the first exploits of police dogs in France. Their introduction completed the resemblance of the police officer to an urban hunter.

The nineteenth century had sketched the portrait of the policeman as a manhunter: "Man," the *Revue Britannique* wrote, "is eminently a hunting animal, but there is no prey that he tracks with such ardor and perseverance as his fellow man. This taste is manifested in such a characteristic way in certain individuals, as soon as they have entered the police, that they are naturally assigned to this special kind of work."[2] The police is a hunting institution, the state's arm for pursuit, entrusted by it with tracking, arresting, and imprisoning.

The police described itself in these terms. Alfonse Bertillon, a proponent of investigative police work based on anthropometric identification, saluted, at the very end of the nineteenth century, "a first step towards a scientific police system, in which all the technical information connected with the manhunt will be brought together in a scientific way. . . . Have not hunters in all ages been incited by information connected with natural history, and, inversely, do not naturalists have something of the hunter's instinct? No doubt the police of the future will come to apply the rules of anthropology to their particular kind of hunting."[3] Thus we move from empirical hunting to scientific tracking. If geography "is useful first of all for war," anthropology is useful first of all for manhunting.

These projects of making hunting practices rational and scientific are the outcome of a long historical process of the state's centralization of the functions of tracking and capture. Unlike hunts for wolf-men, the state hunts by the police no longer take place in the mode of a popular operation of flushing out the prey. The police has gained a monopoly on legitimate tracking. Neither do these state hunts imply the subsequent proscription of the fugitive. Whereas in the older model, setting outside the law was a structural procedure, modern police tracking is, on the contrary, *supposed* to remain within the strict framework of the law. The police as a power of tracking is presented as the instrument and servant of the law.

But the problem is that, far from coming into being as a second application of the law or as an authority originally subordinate to it, the cynegetic power inherited by the modern police force developed largely outside the judicial framework that now justifies it. So although the police officially justifies its existence by constant reference to the legal system and to the law, in practice it remains largely blind. Bertillon is very clear on this subject: the police make no use of the legal system; therefore it is pointless to inflict elaborate legal training on them. Of what utility would that be to them? "Now legal learning always has been and always will be primarily the attribute of magistrates, who know the law better than anybody else. But what a difference when we go on to the application! While the justice should execute only what the law commands him to do, all means are useful to the police that can aid in the discovery of the truth: in the matter of legislation they hardly need to know anything more than the limits beyond which law and custom forbid them to go."[4] Thus, for the police the legal system appears as an external limit set to its activity.

That is because the police, as a power of pursuit, does not deal with legal subjects but rather with bodies in movement, bodies that escape and that it must catch, bodies that pass by and that it must intercept. Whence the antinomy, constantly staged in contemporary cinematic fiction, between the requirements of police pursuit and the principles of the law. To be an efficient hunter, one must pursue the prey despite the law, and even against it. But this antinomy was not born in the imaginations of film scriptwriters. In passing from the law to the police, we pass from one sphere of sovereignty to another, from the theology of the state—the legal system—to its material form—the police. From its spiritual existence to its secular arm. Both deal with the same objects, but from different points of view: subjects without bodies/bodies without subjects.

With the body that it pursues, the police enters into a relationship that is animal-like, even in the affects that it experiences. We must listen to what police officers say, the way they describe what they do: "In their jargon, they say: 'We are the hunters, we're not like the others; they're soldiers.' "[5] A well-guarded secret today, but widely recognized in the nineteenth century: the police do not function out of respect for the law—that is not their main motivation—but because of the pleasure of the hunt. Great authors have acknowledged this. Balzac: "The policeman has all the emotions of the hunter."[6] Maxime du Camp: "People become passionate about this line of work, and that is understandable, for manhunting is, according to those who have practiced it, the most intense of all pleasures."[7] The little secret of police hunts is the pleasure that the officers take in it.

Thus an initial tension or contradiction: if police action finds its main justification in respect for the law, what drives it in practice is something quite different: the desire and the pleasure of the pursuit, in relation to which the law appears as an obstacle to its full development.

But this system of pursuit and capture characteristic of police power is marked by two more great structural contradictions.

In the nineteenth century, the problem was first of all the uncomfortable proximity of the police and delinquency. To track down criminals, one must not only know them but also identify with them, melt into their milieus, adopt their customs, their language, their clothes, their attitudes. This is another great cinematic theme: the mirror relationship between the cop and the criminal, the secret affinity of hunter and hunted, who may go so far as to exchange faces.

One character incarnates par excellence these incestuous relations between the state and crime in the nineteenth century: Vidocq, the former convict who became the chief of the national security police. The preface that precedes his *Memoirs* establishes a direct connection between the aptitudes required for police tracking of criminals and the recruitment of a former convict for this task:

> One cannot imagine how much mental tension and remarkable faculties this manhunting requires. . . . This superior art must be thoroughly possessed by a true policeman, and moreover, like a modern Proteus, he needs to assimilate everything the ignoble habitués of dives and seedy bars have in the way of flexibility, nimbleness, all the marvelous instincts borrowed from cats and serpents. . . . [T]he trickiness, the impenetrable mask of the confirmed criminal, are all gifts indispensable for the clever agent of public power. . . . These exceptional qualities . . . were combined in Vidocq, concentrated to a supreme degree.[8]

The problem is that, to track down delinquents, the police depended on these delinquents themselves, beginning with the agents that it recruited—spies, informers, snitches, turncoats of all kinds. Thus a concern arose: "When thieves hunt thieves, one can never be sure that they won't end up making a deal, and then what becomes of the hunt? . . . It is inconceivable that, in all ages, the police has always employed only degenerates; there are so many decent people!"[9]

Whence also the political hope of disengaging the police from its questionable relationships with the milieu of delinquents: opposing to an artisanal pursuit a scientific pursuit with its own autonomous rationality, relieved of its almost conniving relations with the criminal underworld. Making spies finally superfluous: since the end of the eighteenth century, that has been the leitmotif of projects for reforming police activity. Plans for a scientific police like that of Bertillon are still situated in the desire to rid police activity of its corrupting dependency on the very people it is supposed to track down. Replacing the intimate relations between the police and delinquents with the cold objectivity of the laboratory, replacing the compromising eye of the informer with the slick paper of anthropometric photography. But if so much emphasis is put on this new scientific character, that is because in reality, beneath the utopia of rational control, other more artisanal practices persist, at the center of which is information provided by humans, that is, the use of the delinquent milieu, mobilized for the hunt itself.

The problem is not only that the police associates with and instrumentalizes the delinquent milieu, but also that its action helps organize and structure it. Long before Foucault, nineteenth-century thinkers had noted this structural failure of the prison and emphasized the irony of a hunt that in reality produces the game that it is supposed to hunt down. As a magistrate of the time put it, prison, far from being the space for the moral redemption of the prisoner, functions instead as a place for the corruption of morals and the incubation of delinquency.

> Everyone recognizes that our prisons, far from guaranteeing the social order, are a devouring plague, a center of crime and contagion. Everyone recognizes that the gradual increase in the number of recidivists proceeds, in large measure, from the established custom of randomly putting together prisoners of all ages, conditions, and moralities; a highly imprudent mixture that is frequently dangerous and fertile in all sorts of shameful abuses; in which disgust-

ing relationships deprive the prisoner of the last traces of decency and modesty; in which, in impious conversations, the elders instruct the young, and the most criminal serve as models for the most inexperienced. It is in prisons that great criminals are trained and that the greatest crimes are planned; it is between those who are freed and join together after they get out that are formed those horrible and mysterious associations whose ruses and cleverness defeat all the surveillance practiced by the authorities.[10]

The fact that prison functions as a vast factory of delinquency, maintaining the phenomenon that it is supposed to check, also casts a shadow back on the meaning of police activity: "One might say that police officers maintain and protect criminals in Paris, just as hunters maintain rabbits in a warren, taking one now and then to test, and releasing them for fifteen or twenty days."[11] Or again, as another contemporary points out: "The mutual teaching of vice, fraud, and theft that is organized by the simple fact of common imprisonment in all our houses of detention . . . provides each year, everywhere in France, for the vast rabbit warren in Paris, more criminal and dangerous animals than the police's bloodhounds will ever be able to track."[12] This is the second great contradiction in the system of pursuit and confinement: the vicious circle of the carceral production of delinquency. Confining delinquents no more suppresses delinquency than confining the poor makes poverty disappear—worse, it intensifies it.

Once confined, prisoners have only one idea in mind: escape:

After working for six months, only at night, the intrepid André Fanfan, using several spikes and his fingernails, managed to dig under his bench a tunnel six meters long and opening onto the port. . . . Clever galley-convicts almost all have for their private use what they call the convict's kit: a metal box in the shape of a case that is as inconspicuous as possible and contains especially: a small saw made from a watch spring and called a *bastringue*, a cold chisel, a razor, a sheath knife, a pocket knife, mustaches, fake sideburns, a hairband, a mirror, etc. They usually conceal this indispensable and marvelous kit in the places that are the most difficult to explore.[13]

When the escape was successful, another kind of tracking began: "As soon as an escape is signaled in the prison, three cannon shots announce it publicly. At the same moment, the people in the city and the countryside set out to stop the fugitive convict. . . . Then there is what the locals call a convict-hunt. . . . Posters bearing the fugitive's description are put up everywhere, sent to brigadiers in the *gendarmerie*, etc. The capture of the convict is paid at the rate of twenty-five francs in the city, a hundred francs in the countryside."[14]

The first challenge faced by the police as a cynegetic power is the fugitive. By his ability to escape pursuit, he presents a political danger: revealing to everyone the state's relative impotence. That is what happened in the late nineteenth century, when anarchist bombs were exploding everywhere and the suspects were still at large: "People mocked the policemen's impotence, and a whole passion for this manhunting was reignited," wrote Zola in *Paris*.[15]

In the context of a security power based on the ability of the state to capture dangerous individuals, the insolent flight of bandits or terrorists amounted to a slap in the face as much as to a political crisis.

The state was then sometimes forced to reactivate old models. In 1878, defied by the "bushranger" Ned Kelly, a tragic bandit who roamed the Australian outback clad in improvised armor and ambushing the police officers sent to catch him, the Australian government promulgated a law—the Felons Apprehension Act—authorizing anyone to shoot fugitives on sight.[16] This was a regression—still possible in a police state—to the old schema of hunting wolf-men.

This kind of expedient is dangerous insofar as it signals an acknowledgement of weakness on the part of the sovereign power: the state admits publicly that it cannot, by its own powers, seize the fugitive. But the call for popular mobilization can also, inversely, initiate a process of establishing solidarity between the people and the state confronted by internal enemies. The hunt for new outlaws then becomes a tactic for strengthening police power, in accord with a schema of national unity against a common danger.

The category that is then established is that of the public enemy no. 1. This has ancient origins. Before becoming a category of the law of war, in which the public enemy (*hostis*) and the particular enemy (*inimicus*) are distinguished, it was originally applied, in the Roman context, to the seditious and to those who committed lèse-majesté, to all those who posed a threat to the sovereign power or the prince's person:[17] "Having been declared a public enemy was enough to make any legal procedure moot; everyone in the empire was authorized to put to death the person who had just been identified as such by the Senate."[18] Because he was the sovereign's enemy, everyone had to become his enemy.

This notion had reemerged in social-contract theories, but in a modified form, being defined less in relation to the sovereign than to society and its law. This did not prevent a citizen who had thus become "by his offenses a rebel and traitor to the fatherland"[19] from being executed as a common enemy.

The modern figure of public enemy no. 1 retains a political element. However, this is no longer defined in relation either to the person of the sovereign or to the social contract. The fact that the public enemies of the twentieth century—Dillinger or Mesrine—took on a political significance has to do with the kind of state power that opposed them, which they appeared to challenge directly by the simple fact of escaping it, whatever else the tenor—limited or downright reactionary—of their political consciousness might have been. By openly defeating efforts to track them down, they were in fact committing, for a security state, the equivalent of the crime of lèse-majesté. Thus, there is a mutation of the figure of the public enemy: instead of the one who offends against the sovereign, he becomes the one who defies the tracking power of the police state. Taunting the hunter-state, revealing its inability to provide security even though security has become its supreme justification, is punishable by death. That is why those who do so are shot down in the street when they could have been captured.

There is a profoundly ambiguous connection between the security state and the public enemy no. 1. Dillinger's long time on the run, while it made apparent to everyone the weakness of the American police, also allowed an increase in the latter's power with the creation of a federal apparatus for tracking, the FBI. In the 1930s press, which described Melvin Purvis's pursuit of Dillinger as "the greatest manhunt in the contemporary annals of crime,"[20] the shooting of the fugitives on sight was applauded: "The hunt is on, and many a human mad dog is going to be disposed of in a summary way."[21]

The other great figure of the internal enemy, apart from the bandit, is, throughout the nineteenth century in Europe, the specter of a working-class revolt. In the phases of repression, the army took over from the police and exploited forms of cynegetic war used in a different way in the colonies. When the poor revolted, they were hunted like the natives.[22]

In the nineteenth century, periodically, after every great popular insurrection, the wolves entered the city. In Rouen in 1848, when the last barricades had fallen under bombardment by cannons and the insurgents had withdrawn into the plain, "men carrying game-bags and double-barreled hunting guns were seen indulging in the pleasure of hunting workers."[23] Examples could be multiplied, but at its paroxysm, it was the *Semaine Sanglante* that best illustrated what the manhunts in these wars against insurrections consisted in.

In his studies for the *Arcade Project*, Walter Benjamin recalled an article in the magazine *L'Illustration* on hunting communards during the *Semaine Sanglante*.[24] Here it is:

The struggle in the streets of the city is over. The insurgents have been routed in all their positions. Those who were not killed in combat, taken prisoner, or shot, have all sought safety in flight. Some took refuge in the sewers, others in the quarries of the America quarter, while still others, the most numerous, fled into the Catacombs. . . . Troops entered through the gate of the *barrière d'Enfer*, while other troops solidly occupied the gate opening onto the plain of Montsouris. Then, armed with torches, the soldiers cautiously descended into the immense ossuary. What happened then can easily be imagined.

CHAPTER 9

The Hunting Pack and Lynching

Meute. Formerly: uprising, sedition, military operation (= *émeute*).
From this: hunting expedition, and finally, pack of hunting dogs . . .
from *movere*, put in motion. The initial sense of movement is
preserved in the derivatives *mutin* . . . and *ameuter*, mobilize, excite.
From the French come the German words *Meute*, pack, *Meuter*, rebel,
Meuterei, mutiny.
   Dictionnaire d'étymologie française

In modern life the Hunting Pack has become the Baiting Crowd. We
know cases of lynch-murders, where people suddenly go after one
man. . . . (ADORNO: Pogrom packs!) Obviously that goes back to
this early case of the hunting pack.
   Dialogue between Elias Canetti and
   Theodor W. Adorno

Up to this point, I have discussed mainly manhunts conducted at the behest of identifiable and organized powers: the
government of the masters, pastoral power, monarchical sovereignty, colonial powers, slave-owner power, the state apparatus.
But the history of cynegetic power cannot be reduced to these
cases. There are also situations in which, independent of the im-
petus provided by a central power, a pack sometimes assembles
in spite of itself, sometimes even against itself, for a manhunt.

For there to be a pack, individuals have to gather together. A
pack is a collective being that draws its strength from numbers.

Once caught, the prey will succumb to a multitude of blows or bites: all the pack's members will have killed the prey, but none of them will be the killer. The pack deindividualizes its members. Its unity is merely temporary, however. Once the hunt is over, it disperses.

Gilles Deleuze saw in the pack a case of an aformal, unorganized, nonhierarchical multiplicity, moving and fluid: "In the pack each individual is guided by his companion, and at the same time the positions incessantly vary. . . . That is why the pack is always 'spread out' and its members are always gathered along a boundary. . . . I am connected to the pack by a foot, a hand, a paw, by the anus, by an eye. That is the pack position."[1] But strangely, Deleuze's packs appear to be packs without prey. What he says about the pack as a multiplicity also holds for a swarm of bees or a school of fish, that is, for animal groups that do not presuppose hunting. But the pack, insofar as it designates "a group of animals that hunts together," has its own unity, which is not defined solely by the relative position of each of its members with respect to the others, but also by that of all with respect to the prey they are hunting.

The hunting pack is held together by a unity of action. It is an attack collective, moving rapidly toward a goal on which all its attention is focused: the prey. As Canetti explains, "I use the word 'pack' for men as well as for animals, because it best expresses the joint and swift movement involved, and the concreteness of the goal in view. The pack wants its prey; it wants its blood and its death."[2] The pack is for murder.

Before meaning "a pack of dogs pursuing an animal in the forests," the French term *meute* was first applied to humans, to designate an uprising, a sedition, an insurrection. The *meute* became an *émeute* (riot, uprising). A surprising etymology, in which the *meute* is first human and political before becoming

FIGURE 6. Manhunting in the catacombs. "La chasse à l'homme dans les cata-combes," *L'Illustration*, no. 1477 (17 June 1871).

animal and cynegetic. In the order of the formation of words, it was thus dogs that were first compared to uprisings, and not the other way around. As Canetti also points out, "The Old French *meute* has two meanings: 'rebellion or insurrection' and also 'the hunt.' "[3] This strange conceptual crossing thus leads to placing the *meute* in politics and the politics of *émeutes* in hunting. But what is the connection? What kind of rioting power (*puissance émeutière*) does the hunting *meute* have?

Claude Neal was lynched on 26 October 1934 in Marianna, Florida. Arrested as a suspect in the murder of a nineteen-year-old white woman, Lola Cannidy, the black farmer was intercepted by the mob, wrenched away from the police, and taken captive. What happened next was reconstructed by an investigator: "After taking the nigger to the woods about four miles from Greenwood, they cut off his penis. He was made to eat it. Then they cut off his testicles and made him eat them and say he liked it. . . . Then they sliced his sides and stomach with knives and every now and then somebody would cut off a finger or a toe."[4] Afterward, Neal was burned with a red-hot iron, dragged behind a car, stabbed by the mother of the victim, and hanged near the municipal court.

A newspaper, the *Panama Pilot*, justified the lynching: "to avenge the insult to womanhood. . . . This was the real reason why hundreds of men left their work and joined in the hunt, with only one object in view — to hunt the criminal, find him . . . , and mete unmerciful torture to him, as he did to a young girl."[5]

The nascent social science of the nineteenth century took an interest in phenomena of collective violence. One of the main subjects of these studies of "crowd psychology" or "mob sociology," in addition to the concepts of contagion or imitation used to account for the formation of these collective subjects of a special kind, was the idea that these contemporary phenomena represented an atavistic resurgence of primitive forces or archaic instincts. The theory of the hunting mob developed by Gustave Le Bon perfectly illustrates this kind of approach:

> Our savage, destructive instincts are the inheritance left dormant in all of us from the primitive ages. In the life of the isolated individual it would be dangerous for him to gratify these instincts, while his absorption in an irresponsible crowd, in which in consequence he is assured of impunity, gives him entire liberty to follow them. . . . The passion, so widespread, for the chase and the

acts of ferocity of crowds proceed from one and the same source. A crowd which slowly slaughters a defenseless victim displays a very cowardly ferocity; but for the philosopher this ferocity is very closely related to that of the huntsmen who gather in dozens for the pleasure of taking part in the pursuit and killing of a luckless stag by their hounds.[6]

The question of manhunts as forms of collective mobilization is thus constantly raised in terms of the enigmatic resurgence or mysterious relapse into a primitive barbarity. So the riddle can be formulated this way: how can archaic violence reemerge at the very heart of civilization? But the problem is that by framing the question in that way we prevent ourselves from answering it. If we begin by presupposing, in accord with a linear philosophy of progress, that "civilization" (the present) excludes barbarity (the past), we cannot avoid a later collision with the recognition of an incomprehensible anachronism. Positing that barbarity is outside civilization, in a kind of chronological evolutionism, prevents us from grasping the contemporary aspect of barbarity, the way in which it may continue to inhabit "civilization," even as its hidden condition.

In one of his last speeches, on the subject of lynching, Frederick Douglass replied to those who, on reading the unbearable account of these acts of violence, asked in good faith: how could normal, civilized men commit such atrocities? After having revealed the implicit idea that this question expresses (namely, if such punitive atrocities are committed, that is probably because the victims are in some way to blame, because no civilized human community would inflict such punishments, with such unanimity, on perfectly innocent people), he says that normal people in the southern states are not normal in the same way as ordinary people: these men and women have been shaped by the institutions of a slave-owning culture, they have been accustomed for centuries to hold the sole power, uninhibited by law, and since childhood they have been brought up to have contempt for Negroes' lives, being certain of their racial supremacy:

> No man can reason correctly on this question who reasons on the assumption that the lynchers are like ordinary men. We are not, in this case, dealing with men in their natural condition, but with men brought up in the exercise of arbitrary power. We are dealing with men whose ideas, habits and customs are entirely different from those of ordinary men. . . . [T]he rules resting upon the justice and benevolence of human nature do not apply to the mobocrats, or to those who were educated in the habits and customs of a slave-holding community. What these habits are I have a right to know, both in theory any in practice. . . . We must remember that these people have not now and have never had any such respect for human life as is common to other men. They have had among them for centuries a peculiar institution, and that peculiar institution has stamped them as a peculiar people.[7]

What Douglass is pointing to here is the *continuum* of violence in racist societies. The violent eruption of lynching is not a thunderbolt in a tranquil sky; it is the culmination of a normality consisting of a constant and multiform disrespect for the life of the dominated. It is connected with a whole fabric of violent acts, with a whole mental landscape, as well as with an age-old series of beatings, humiliations, and murders. Thus, the question here is not how to understand that normality suddenly becomes an exception to itself or how civilized people relapse into barbarity. Instead, we have to ask what makes it possible, in the historical and social texture of this very normality, for a bundle of threads to suddenly form a knot: the event of lynching. Feminists have proposed a theory of the continuum of sexist violence. The thesis holds equally well for racist violence.

In lynching, human packs appear as the agents of popular vengeance, an immanent form of "justice" that is exercised contrary to the judicial institution, in a system of action entirely foreign to the legal system and the law. It is a kind of punishment without investigation, an execution without a law, without prosecution or legal forms, an unauthorized punishment inflicted without regard for actual responsibility or proof. If hunting packs have an insurrectional power, that is because their aggressive movement and violence short-circuits the institutional violence of the authorities and the state. It is a mutiny against the legal order, against the institutional forms of punishment.

The prison was attacked, the courtroom was invaded to seize the prey. But if the state's authority was flouted, that was nonetheless done with the state's complicity: the authorities rarely intervened to prevent an anticipated lynching, and it was even more exceptional for the lynchers to be punished for their acts. The practice was in fact tolerated, since it remained largely unpunished. The surest sign of a system of racist hunting is that the authors of the violent acts are never called to account—an impunity that amounts to a license to murder.

By reappropriating, against the law, police and penal prerogatives, the lynch mob reaffirms itself as the real and original power behind the legal power, the primordial and always reactivatable source of the constitutive power. Behind the formal power of institutions and the law, there is a group from which everything derives: the caste of white men, the substance of the state.

But such a demonstration of force requires, in order for power to manifest itself, an exceptional crime, a transgression that, by its odious character, demands in response an immediate departure from the normal order of justice. The typical accusation that made this possible was the rape of a white woman: "This charge once fairly started, no matter by whom or in what manner, whether well or ill-founded, whether true or false, is certain to subject the accused to immediate death."[8] Frederick Douglass shows again how this accusation, which was at first nonexistent, later came to be substituted for the charges of sedition that previously justified lynching blacks. In a parallel way, in the racist mentality the black man became the archetype of the sexual aggressor.[9] Having become the exclusive attribute of black men, insulting and raping women justified, in turn, the outbreak of racist violence on the part of white men. By using the emblem of the white woman to be defended and avenged, men of the white caste could present themselves "as protectors of civilization, reaffirming not only their role as social and familial 'heads,' but their paternal property rights as well."[10]

Archeologically speaking, the *pater familias* alone has the right to decide whether members of his family live or die. This power has been challenged by the aggression and he has to reaffirm it. That is what explains the refusal to leave it to the state to handle the matter. Heads of families have to demonstrate that they still have this power. This involves publicly punishing the suspect. Beyond the simple logic of the *lex talionis*, an eye for an eye, the practices of emasculation that accompany lynchings[11] serve to reassert in the most literal way that white men, and they alone, possess the phallus. Lynching allows the restoration of the power of the fathers and the reterritorialization, through the intermediary of the hunting pack, of the political community of the patriarchal family.

A lyncher in Georgia explained:

I reckon folks from the north think we're hard on niggers, but they just don't know what would happen to the white people if the niggers ran wild like they would if we didn't show them who's boss. . . . There's a lot of fine ones in this country, but they're the ones who know how to keep their place, and they don't make trouble. This nigger that raped that white girl is a mean one. Of course, that girl is a whore, and everybody knows it, and for all I know she led him on, but just the same she was a white girl, and he was a nigger, and it just wouldn't do to let him go. That's why we're out here trying to jump him in the woods. . . . I've got niggers working for me, and I get along the best way with them, because they know how to keep their place. If that nigger out there in the woods gets jumped before the sheriff finds him, it will all be over and done with by sundown, and everybody will be satisfied.[12]

We understand that as he sees it, the problem is not so much the rape—we find a whole set of sexist platitudes in this case—as that the alleged rapist is black and the woman is white. The accusation of rape calls for lynching if and only if the color line has been crossed in the direction from black to white. Attacking a white woman when one is a black—or being suspected of doing so, which amounts to the same thing—is the sign that one does not "know one's place." The notion that the Negro has to "know his place" and its implicit corollary, that Negroes *stay* in their place, is the condition for whites' retaining their place, namely their place as the dominant racial caste.

It is enough that people believe—that whites believe, but also and perhaps especially that blacks believe—that a black man has been able to touch a white woman with impunity for a threat to be posed to the order of domination based on the principle of the nonreversibility of violence between dominant and dominated. As soon as such a thing is believed, a dangerous possibility has opened up that has to be denied with the most implacable force. That is also why the actual guilt of the suspect is an absolutely negligible question for the lynch mob.

Here, beyond putting individuals to death, the goal of the hunting pack is not—as in other historical forms—the expulsion or massacre of the prey-group, but rather its maintenance within the narrow limits of a social domination by race. On the bodies hanged from trees, the lynchers sometimes left signs as a warning to blacks who passed by. Lynching is a call to order addressed to the dominated. As Oliver C. Cox put it, "By lynching, Negroes are kept in their place, that is to say, kept as a great, easily-exploitable, common-labor reservoir. . . . [L]ynching and the threat of lynching is the fundamental reliance of the white ruling class in maintaining the status quo. It is a sub-legal contrivance developed to meet a vital social need, which, because of the powerful democratic conventions of Western society, cannot be satisfied by formal law."[13]

Lynching is one of the historically neglected cases of the insurrection of the dominant group against the dominated. It is a riot (*émeute*) by the masters against their former slaves for the purpose of perpetuating the relationship of domination.

In the same period, other racial packs were formed elsewhere, which, beyond the apparent similarities—a man, darker-skinned than the others, runs to escape from a crowd of pursuers—are governed by quite different dynamics.

CHAPTER 10

Hunting Foreigners

In addition, there are many reflections to be made on this hunt for
foreign workers; but we shall add only this: it is necessary that the
workers, the proletarians of all countries, recognize each other as
brothers, that is, as all and everywhere equally wretched, and therefore all and everywhere in solidarity against the exploiters.

FRÉDÉRIC FROBEN (TAILOR), PETER WARTENS (CABINET-
MAKER), AND PHILIPP REPPNER (TANNER), *L'ATELIER*

ON 16 AUGUST 1893, at a work site in the region of Aigues-
Mortes in southern France, an Italian worker dipped his dirty
shirt in a reservoir of water intended for drinking. A fight between French and Italian workers resulted. But things did not
stop there: "The news of this attack soon spread to the various
work sites. . . . The workers banded together. Armed with shovel
handles, around 4 a.m. they set out on a veritable manhunt."[1]
The authorities decided to evacuate the Italian workers: "The
French followed our column, throwing stones and shouting,

"Death to the Italians! Go back to Crispi's! We want your blood!" . . .
[A] column of about four hundred demonstrators appeared, pre-
ceded by two flags, one a tricolor and the other red, on which had
been written in Italian: "Death to Italians! Today we are going to
make sausage of them!" . . . The furious Frenchmen attacked with

109

sticks those who lagged behind . . . trampling them and showering them with stones. One of these unfortunates, a man from Turin, thinking he might save himself, stood up with his face running blood and cried: "Leave me alone, I'm Corsican, I'm French! Save me! This was of no help to him. He was hit by stones and beaten with sticks and fell dead in the middle of the road."[2]

By evening, there were dozens of dead and injured. The next day the mayor of Aigues-Mortes made an official announcement: "The Company withdraws all work from those of Italian nationality."

In manhunts that take the form of mob violence, a clear political goal is pursued: expulsion. People cry "kill him!" and killing in fact takes place, but if they murder someone, it is in order to expel him. The leitmotif of lynchings was: "The Negro has to stay in his place"; that of xenophobic hunts is: "Foreigners out!" The former are racist hunts of segregation, the latter xenophobic hunts of exclusion. The mob demands both that immigrants be expelled from the city and that they be denied work.

Even if the hostility is expressed in terms of national oppositions—French versus Italians, with all the usual clichés—the antagonism is primarily social. Hunts for foreigners are hunts for foreign *workers*. After the events at Aigues-Mortes, Napoleone Colajanni showed how inappropriate the expression "hunting Italians" was, not only because other minorities had also been the targets of comparable acts of violence, but also and especially because, in every case, "this hunt was carried out at the expense of workers of the lowest category." And he added: "if in France hatred and political resentment existed in depth and were generally widespread, they would be shown above all against our cultivated classes." Since this was not the case, "it seems to me possible to conclude that national hatred and resentment have little to do with the sad events at Aigues-Mortes, at least as essential motives."[3]

The root of this violence was to be sought less in national hatred than in the competition for jobs between two labor groups of different national origins.[4] Xenophobic hunts arise from competition for wages. Their logic involves interpredation: the exploited against the exploited, the poor against the poor, workers against workers.

Although capitalism did not invent xenophobic violence, it has channeled it toward the powerful interpredatory dynamics that characterizes it. In so doing, it has also endowed it with a redoubtable social power. Certain political movements soon understood this.

In 1893, right after the events at Aigues-Mortes, the conservative French press, condemning "these cut-rate workers who come to our work sites to take bread out of Frenchmen's mouths," demanded that "a high tariff be put on the harmful, adulterated merchandise that is brought into the country and is known as the Italian worker."[5] Echoing this agitation, in Paris homemade posters appeared, calling for a hunt for foreigners: "We are invaded by foreigners. The little work that exists is being done by Germans, Italians, Belgians, etc. . . . Come on, comrades, let's follow the example of our brothers in Aigues-Mortes and Nancy and drive out the foreigners. Let's show that it is French blood that flows in our veins."[6]

Symptomatically, it was also in that year that Maurice Barrès, the spiritual father of national socialism, published his pamphlet *Against Foreigners: A Study for the Protection of French Workers.*[7] In it, Barrès advocated protectionism for the national labor market. The same rhetoric is found five years later in his electoral campaign program: "Even on work sites where he competes with French workers, the foreigner, like a parasite, poisons us. There is one essential principle that must guide the new French policy, and that is protecting all French nationals against this invasion."[8]

Protection, that is the new key word: "If we want the product to be protected, it is in order to protect the national producer, the management and the workers. And that leads us to measures to favor the French worker over the foreigner working in France."[9] Extending protectionism from products to workers, that is the fundamental move by which the conservative and nationalist right sought, over the course of the second half of the nineteenth century, to transform popular xenophobia into a political program. Its twin mottoes became the expulsion of foreigners and preference for French nationals.

This political operation was carried out by extreme right-wing theoreticians at the very time that in the 1880s, against the background of an economic crisis, outbreaks of xenophobic violence were occurring in the working class. Just as socialism had recognized in strikes the social power that could help it emerge as a political force, reactionary and conservative nationalism, which was both racist and anti-Semitic, saw in hunting down and expelling foreign workers its practical counterpart and, at the same time, the ferment, the potential power of mobilization for its conquest of power.

To treat the circulation of workers in the same way that merchandise was being treated, that is, to treat human beings as things, was an idea that had been discussed much earlier, but by others. In the mid-1840s, the economist Frédéric Bastiat, whose liberal notions had been criticized by the editors of the workers' periodical *L'Atelier*, replied by pointing out an apparent contradiction in their discourse: how could they accept the use of protectionism against foreign merchandise and reject it against foreign workers?

What is one protecting in France? Things that are made by big business in huge factories, iron, oil, textiles. . . . However, every time foreign labor seeks to enter our market in a form that can harm you but helps big business, isn't it allowed to come in? Aren't there thirty thousand Germans making clothing and shoes in Paris? Why are they permitted to work alongside you when we reject textiles? . . . We are not asking that German tailors and English roadworkers be expelled. We are asking that they be allowed to come in on the same terms as textiles and rails. We are demanding justice for all, equality before the law for all."[10]

The clever trick here consisted in reformulating, for the occasion, free-trade positions in socialist rhetoric. First, Bastiat adopts the theme of equality, but in a very special sense in which "equality for all" henceforth means, in a very extended sense, the equality of things and persons—merchandise necessarily enjoying, by virtue of this principle, the same freedom of circulation as workers.[11] Then he uses the vocabulary of social justice, going so far as to denounce the double standard adhered to by bourgeois protectionists who expose their workers to competition while at the same time rejecting it for themselves. Here he employs an argument by reductio ad absurdum: for him, it is not a matter of rejecting the free circulation of workers; on the contrary, he bases himself on the self-evidence of this freedom in order to found, by analogy, that of commerce. It was an ingenious argument. But it was dangerous, because it amounted to positing indirectly the closure of the national labor market and the exclusion of foreigners as the sole conceivable alternative to putting workers into capitalist competition.

The conservative right soon grasped the flaw in the argument, understanding that it offered a major ideological opportunity. Adopting the debate's presuppositions, in the late 1840s it began to demand the expulsion of foreign labor in the name of a nationalist protectionism for labor.[12] By an irony of history, what had appeared in liberal discourse as a paradoxical argument designed to convert the labor movement to free trade, had provided first the conservative right, and then the racist and anti-Semitic far right, with the matrix principle of their political programs.

Set up in this way, in the form of a simple choice between free trade and protectionism, the question was loaded from the outset. In such a framework, the object to be protected immediately became national, and the foreigner the threat to it. Bastiat's question, "What are we protecting?" nonetheless remains pertinent *in one sense*: who should be the subject of protection? But also: What is the threat? From whom must we be protected? These are questions that are foreclosed when the debate is formulated as an opposition between free trade and nationalist protectionism.

The demands for social protection made by the labor movement—the very ones that were at the source of the advances in labor law and systems of collective solidarity—had clearly identified the main threat: capitalist exploitation of labor at the expense of workers' lives. In contrast, by a process of displacement and condensation, the identification of protection with the defense of national interests made the foreigner the center and incarnation of all threats. It was then no longer from abuses by management that the workers had to be protected, but rather from themselves, or rather from a part of themselves that had been redefined as their enemy. The effect of this displacement was to redraw the mental and real map of the opposing camps, to play one political identification off against another, national identity against class consciousness. The procedure was radical, and radically dangerous, because it transformed at a fundamental level the very terms of politics, that is, the definition of friend and enemy, the way the pertinent oppositions and antagonisms were conceived.

The founding act of xenophobic politics is the drawing of this boundary line between those who have to be protected and those who can—or rather, must—be excluded from protection. Political xenophobia is defined by this operation of demarcation whose matrix, as we have just seen, was borrowed from the discourse of economics. Biological racism merges with this apparatus in order to define the essence of what deserves to be protected, in order to give a substantial content to the concept of the national. But what has to be understood is that the definition of identity by race is not indispensable for the functioning of this apparatus. Cultural or historical definitions will do just as well. National identity is a blank that can be filled in various ways, insofar as the positive determination of what it is to be "national" is only a secondary element in the mechanism of exclusion that is set up here. In other words, one of the lessons of this genealogy is that xenophobic exclusion as a political program does not presuppose the theory of races: theories of identity determine only secondarily the empty terms in a structure of exclusion that is politically anterior to them. That is also why the—necessary—refutations of racist ideologies are by themselves powerless to thwart xenophobia as a system of political exclusion. It does not suffice to say that these ideologies posit as natural what are in fact only factitious entities, beings consisting in fantasies and discourse, without autonomous substance. One also has to be able to oppose to them alternative systems of political identification, other notions of protection, of what must be protected, other political categories of collective protection from relationships of predation.

To Bastiat, the editors of *L'Atelier* replied: "We do not ask that foreign workers who come to work in France be expelled, not even on the pretext of protecting national labor."[13] But they based their rejection entirely on an invocation of moral values, on the idea that altruistic considerations should take priority over economic interests: "We understand very well that their work diminishes our own, that our salaries must be eroded by their competition; but that is not what we care about most; in that respect . . . we do not imitate the example set by a certain class that puts profit above everything."[14] Next, their argument was founded on a kind of open patriotism: those who remained would become French, and as for those who left, they would "still be ours to a certain extent," because through contact with "us" they would have assimilated "our ideas, our doctrines." The authors thus made use of a concept of fraternity inherited from both the cosmopolitanism of the Enlightenment and the discourse of the French Revolution: France, the incarnation and center of the universal. But formulated in this way, their arguments were very thin. If the xenophobic option was rejected, it was in the name of a conception that was generous, to be sure, but almost impotent on the political level, because it was incapable of responding on the terrain on which Bastiat, in a strictly tactical maneuver, had located himself, namely on that of class interests. These republican workers thus put themselves in a difficult and dangerous position: having begun by conceding that their class interest was indeed to support the xenophobic closure of the labor market, they were left with nothing to oppose to the power of that economic interest but the moral values of the fatherland and the rights of man.

In 1848, between two revolutions, expulsions of foreign workers took place in Paris.[15] The workers', republican, and progressive press immediately published reactions condemning these "selfish manifestations" and also emphasizing that they were carried out by a very small minority.

One group of German immigrant workers wrote to the editors of *L'Atelier* to congratulate them on their protest "against efforts, as unjust as they are imprudent, made by a few persons whose idea is to expel foreign workers and office workers from Paris."[16] Their letter developed a whole argument against the temptations of "nationalistic exclusivism": "The expulsion of foreigners," they wrote, "would be very detrimental in several respects: (1) It would defy in a terrifying way the sacred motto *Fraternity* that is inscribed on all monuments and decrees. (2) It would anger, not foreign governments, but foreign peoples against the French people. . . . (3) It would advance the situation of the French worker not at all; for if there are some 200,000 workers in Paris, and you expel the 50,000 who are foreign . . . would not the gap . . . left by the departure of a fourth of them soon be filled by French people from the provinces?"[17] A combination, then, of moral, pragmatic, and economic arguments.

However, the authors added to this argument an appeal that belonged to an entirely different register of political discourse: "It is necessary that the workers, the proletarians of all countries, recognize each other as brothers, that is, as all and everywhere equally wretched, and therefore all and everywhere in solidarity against the exploiters; for us workers, that is the sad and lugubrious meaning of the word *fraternity*; but it also implies the hope of a great and sublime universal rehabilitation of proletarians in all countries."[18]

We see, by contrast, the originality but also the strength of their position: their argument consisted in saying that it was still and especially class interest itself, by virtue of its orientations rightly understood, that motivated their opposition to xenophobic exclusion. The pertinent argument was not that thanks to the free circulation of people French workers were going to be able to spread the spirit of emancipation throughout the world, nourishing foreigners on the milk of "our" principles—an idea that unfortunately reflected a very chauvinistic arrogance—but rather that nationalistic exclusivism produced a deleterious division of the working class, preventing it from uniting in its battle against a common enemy.

In this new schema, the exploited had to "*recognize each other* as brothers." Fraternity no longer has the immediacy of an essence but the necessity of a mutual recognition. However, the latter no longer involves the essence of a common *identity*, but rather the awareness of the similarity of the *situations experienced*. What constitutes the common element is neither an origin nor a determinate identity but a condition, a shared social position, an experience that can be transposed. In this new conception of fraternity, people *become* brothers—or sisters—not by filiation or birth, but by the simple fact of recognizing their own situation in that of the other.

The underlying philosophical question is that of the political subject's mode of existence: defining the collective subject, not in a substantialist manner, but through a set of intersecting identifications in which people recognize one another by what they have in common, negatively: their situations. The shared condition that founds mutual recognition here is a negative situation, that of exploitation. Whence also the "sad and lugubrious meaning" of this new notion of fraternity, which loses the immediate innocence that it could still have in bourgeois universalism. If it now takes on a bitter meaning, that is because it bonds together brothers in misfortune. But this negative unity then takes on another aspect, that of a struggle. Brothers in misery become brothers in arms. From that point on, it is no longer solely in the name of the universal equality of persons that nationalistic exclusivism is rejected, but also in the name of a solidarity with strategic implications: beyond national boundaries, the fraternity of class founds a combative unity. Because this notion is incompatible with both liberal competition and nationalistic exclusion on the labor market, by rejecting the terms of an imposed alternative it makes it possible to fight on two fronts, against free-traders and against xenophobes. The point is not to defend national workers against the competition of foreign workers, but to defend all workers against being put into capitalist competition. To oppose to competition that divides, not nationalistic exclusion, but social solidarity.

The German workers' formulations echoed too literally those of the *Manifesto of the Communist Party*, which had been published in German in London just two months earlier, for us not to see in them a direct influence. That would mean that the first use, the first direct political application of the *Manifesto's* formulas, was made in Paris by immigrant workers, in order to oppose expulsions of foreigners. Thus the alternative was posed very early on: class struggle or xenophobic hunts.

At the end of the nineteenth century, Bernard Lazare, an enemy of anti-Semitism and all forms of racism and a determined adversary of Barrès, perfectly understood the meaning of the ideological maneuvers that were underway on the far right, and also what their historical outcome might be: "Beware of this patriotic egoism, this nationalistic protectionism; it will cost you dearly someday: that's what they'll use to bleed you dry. Beware of the pseudo-socialists who tell you that if your wages are low, foreign workers and Jews are to blame, and that you will be better off once both of them have been expelled. How the bourgeois would laugh if he could get you to fight your comrades in misery, your companions on the chain gang, and in that way save his own skin."[19]

CHAPTER 11

Hunting Jews

"Would you hunt men?" I asked him.
"We will find them wherever they are hidden."
INTERVIEW CONDUCTED BY PASTOR MARC BOEGNER,
PRESIDENT OF LA CIMADE, WITH PIERRE LAVAL,
9 SEPTEMBER 1942

IN 1320, the Pastoureaux[1] launched their second crusade in Languedoc. "Continuing to wage war and to hunt down Jews,"[2] they entered Toulouse. A resident, Baruch l'Allemand, described the event:

These Pastoureaux and the crowd then invaded the Jewish quarter. I was in my room, studying and writing, when these people came to my house and began to shout: "Death, death, get baptized or we'll kill you immediately." Seeing the fury of this crowd, and seeing that they were killing before my eyes other Jews who refused to be baptized, I replied that I would prefer that to being killed. They then seized me, made me leave the house without allowing me to take other clothes or anything at all, and took me just as I was to the cathedral of Saint-Étienne. When I got there, two clerics showed me a few bodies of Jews lying in front of the church, and told me: "If you don't get baptized, you will have to die, like those whom you see here."[3]

The history of the European Jews is one of age-old persecutions. Since the Middle Ages, there have been repeated episodes of manhunting: beatings, arson, expulsions, massacres. Considering these scenes of violence one after another makes one feel one is stuttering, so much do the images, the gestures, the slogans, resemble one another from one century to the next.

However, Hannah Arendt warned us against the idea of an "eternal anti-Semitism" that is fixed and without history. Apart from the fact that this thesis explains nothing, it involves a political danger: that of absolving the perpetrators of violent acts by invoking something that transcends European history. In her view, the theory of the scapegoat is equally problematic: as a theory of an outlet for violence that chooses its victims in an arbitrary way (it could have been anyone else), this pseudo-explanation leads people in reality to "escape the seriousness of anti-Semitism and the significance of the fact that the Jews were driven into the storm center of events."[4] Combined, these two ideas lead to the conclusion that if the Jews were chosen as victims, it is basically because it was always natural that they would be. Arendt emphasized, on the contrary, the historical nature of these phenomena, refusing to merge them in a general and eternal model. Her hypothesis was that the reasons for modern anti-Semitism were to be sought conjointly in a history of the social function of Jews and the formation and then crisis of nation-states.

In the course of their history, hunts for Jews went schematically through three major mutations: hunts by mobs, then hunts by states; religious hunts, then racist hunts; murderous hunts, then genocidal hunts. These three mutations are connected.

The first historical model is that of the crusade-hunt. The hunts conducted by the Pastoureaux are an example of this. They are mob hunts. Whatever their other roots might be, they

FIGURE 7a. Hunting Jews in the Frankfurt ghetto in 1614 (engraving made in 1642). Engraving by H. Merian, taken from J. L. Gottfried, *Historische Chronica* (Frankfurt: n.p., 1642), p. 1142.

are expressed through religious hunts. Their ideology is that of Christian anti-Judaism, directed against the "deicide people." Their motto is: "Conversion or death." Even if this alternative was purely rhetorical and led in fact to massacres, the hunt was presented as a means of conversion, a proselytizing hunt that was going to "compel them to come in" by violent means. The line of demarcation between the hunters and their prey was that of religious faith, which was to be professed or abjured.

In this hunt for pagans, Christian identity left those outside it only one alternative: convert or disappear. But of course conversion itself was also a way of disappearing, disappearing by absorption and indifferentiation. In this case, elimination and assimilation are the two inseparable terms of a single alternative, the two means of action available for a force whose horizon is to become the totality: either you are us or you are nothing.

FIGURE 7b. The anti-Semitic "Hep-Hep" riots in 1819. Engraving by Johann Michael Voltz. "Hep! hep!" was the rallying cry for anti-Semitic rioters. A fanciful etymology traces it back to the Crusades, seeing it as the acronym of a Latin formula: "Hierusalem Est Perdita"—"Jerusalem is lost." It is more likely to be a deformation of the German "Hebe! Hebe!" –"Stop him! Catch him!" In 1819, the Hep-Hep riots ignited reactions in Europe from Wurzburg to Copenhagen and Amsterdam.

The flip side of assimilation is the suppression of those who refuse to come in. Thus, we have another variant of the pastoral hunt. Even though this time it is expressed in terms of forced inclusion rather than excommunication, it is still based on the same fundamental postulate: outside of us there is nothing but death. This holds for those who are expelled from the community and have to die, and also for the spectral figures who roam the periphery of the real world—the Christian world—and who have to make up their minds to come in or to disappear.

Confronted with such an alternative, in the most extreme situations resistance was reduced to the freedom to die: committing suicide to deprive the enemy of his power of killing. In

1320, a group of Jews fleeing the approach of the Pastoureaux found refuge in a fortified tower in Verdun-sur-Garonne. The assailants besieged them: it is alleged that "the besieged defended themselves with great courage; and after having thrown all kinds of stones and beams on their enemies, and everything they could find, they threw their own children on them. Finally the Pastoureaux, having assembled a great quantity of wood and set fire to the tower's gate, all the Jews, whom the smoke made very uncomfortable, seeing that there was no other hope of saving themselves, made the extreme decision to kill each other rather than die at the hands of the Pastoureaux."[5]

Seen from a strategic angle, anti-Semitic hunts have long had the function of diverting attention from political antagonisms. David Nirenberg has shown how anti-Semitic riots in the Middle Ages were, in reality, situated in a more complex way in the framework of a revolt against monarchical power. The Pastoureaux, he explains, "saw the Jews as fiscal agents of the state, which some Jews were. . . . They knew, too, that Jews were under the king's protection."[6] In other words, these riots were also "a rebellion against royal fiscality, camouflaged with the very language of sacred monarchy and Crusade."[7] In Christian society, the Jews as a group had been in part forced to occupy a social function that was both economically necessary and religiously prohibited, that of providing credit and usury. As Michelet summed it up, "during the Middle Ages, persecuted, driven out, brought back, they were the indispensable intermediary between the tax officials and the latter's' victims, between the agent and the patient, taking money from those below and delivering it to the king above."[8] But this ascending function of financial extraction, of which credit and taxation were the instruments, was accompanied by a second function that was descending and political: identified as subordinate parts of the machinery of royal taxation, the Jews served as convenient targets for antitax revolts, which, rather than attack the central power directly, targeted the social group that was connected with the latter—the king's serfs, the Jews. What then took place was that the revolt against the state was displaced onto a subordinate social group.

But much later on, when this economic function had disappeared as a specific trait and the figure of the Jewish usurer was no more than an ideological vestige, the stereotype of a rigid racist imagery, the strategic function of anti-Semitism as a displacement of social anger did not disappear. Bernard Lazare, reflecting on the reasons for the persecutions of Jews in Russia in the nineteenth century, has described the mechanism:

> What are then the real causes of antisemitism? . . . The Russian people, laden with misery, crushed under taxes, groaning under the most atrocious of tyrannies, embittered by administrative violence and governmental abuse of power, burdened with suffering and humiliation, is in an unbearable condition. Generally resigned, they are liable to yield to passions; their uprisings and revolts are formidable; antisemitic riots are the proper thing to divert popular anger, and that is why the government encouraged them and often provoked them. As to the peasants and workingmen, they fell upon the Jews because, they said, "the Jew and the nobleman are of a pair, only it is easy to thrash the Jew." . . . Thus is explained the plundering of rich Jewish merchants, of wealthy money-lenders, often of poor Jewish workmen, and it is heart-rending to see these disinherited fall upon one another instead of uniting against the oppressive tsarism.[9]

If the hunts undertaken by modern anti-Semitism are still expressed partly in the classical vocabulary of religious anti-Judaism, their motto is no longer "conversion or death," but "expulsion or death": "Hepp! Hepp! Hepp! Death and ruin to all Jews, you have to flee or die."[10] In this new alternative, the hunt is no longer presented as a means of forcible conversion but as bloody exclusion. As a contemporary newspaper explained, the Hep-hep rioters were "merchants, educated people who were prepared to pardon the Jews their disbelief and Asiatic origin if only they would stay out of wholesale and retail trade in English and French products and return to their old commodities."[11] The corporatist expulsion of the Jews, their economic expulsion, was what the anti-Semitic mobs wanted, and that is what they got: "The caste of merchants and the craft guilds that had fomented the riots had attained its goal: the Senate strengthened measures excluding Jews from branches of craft activity that were governed by the guilds."[12]

Modern anti-Semitism was above all a petit-bourgeois ideology. At the beginning of the twentieth century, it became the privileged political expression of the rigid and inconsistent anticapitalism of a petite bourgeoisie which, against the background of an economic crisis, distinguished between good industrial capital and bad financial capital, good national capital and bad foreign capital, making the "Jew" the incarnation of what was harmful in the power of money. Anti-Semitism then appeared as a way of formulating a vague anticapitalist sentiment while channeling it, in a socially comfortable way, toward the phantasmatic representatives of a certain form of capital: "The irony of history," wrote Abram Leon in the middle of World War II,

wills that the most radical anti-Semitic ideology in all history should triumph precisely in the period when Judaism is on the road of economic and social assimilation. But like all "ironies of history" this seeming paradox is very understandable. At the time when the Jew was unassimilable, at a time when he really represented "capital," he was indispensable to society. There could be no question of destroying him. At the present time, capitalist society, on the edge of the abyss, tries to save itself by resurrecting the Jew and the hatred of the Jews. But it is precisely because the Jews do not play the role which is attributed to them that anti-Semitic persecution can take on such an amplitude.[13]

Whereas anti-Semitic hunting had historically served state power as a safety valve, at the dawn of the twentieth century the new strategic project of extreme right-wing movements was to mobilize it against the existing state apparatuses, to intensify the power of political subversion exercised by such hunting packs and to turn around what had long functioned as a safety belt for state authority to make it a means of seizing state power. But if their strategy later proved to be historically capable of attracting a crucial fraction of the dominant social strata, that was also because in doing so its function of diverting social antagonisms did not disappear: it smothered the class struggle by means of race war, even at the price of destroying the old forms of state power.

Just as it theorized hunting the foreigner, at the end of the nineteenth century the far right also theorized hunting Jews. This was logically consistent, moreover, because in its view "the Jew" represented the foreigner of the worst kind.

In *La France juive*, Drumont denounces the insidious conquest that is supposed to have allowed Jews to invade all the important positions in society and to drive all the French out of them, beginning with the estates and chateaus of the old aristocracy.[14] In a passage titled "Jewish Hunts: The Stag's Revenge," he gives an emotional description of the torments of the stag who used to be hunted by the French nobility, before explaining what its revenge would now consist in: "Isn't the unfortunate stag avenged, after being tracked down century after century, by the sight of all these bearers of great names trudging along, under the ironic gaze of the huntsmen, behind some disgusting Jew from Germany or Russia . . . ? These forests where the ancestors rode, the bold conquerors of old Gaul, black with woods, are still haunted by the legends of the past. . . . Fontainebleau belongs to Ephrussi, Versailles to Hirsch, Ferrières to Rothschild."[15] The social decline of the old aristocracy and the intrusion of Jewish hunters on its former domains—that is supposed to be vengeance for the animals of the forest. In his racist vision, Drumont also immediately makes these "Jewish hunts" manhunts—going so far as to claim that Hirsch told his gamekeepers: "As soon as you see Frenchmen, shoot into the crowd!"[16]

Reciprocally, in the anti-Semitic imagination, reconquering the lost power involves reappropriating the manly privilege of hunting. To reverse the decline, to be the masters once again, the "French" had to become hunters again—but hunters of Jews. Céline, denouncing in turn the internal colonization of the country by "Jewish *négrites*," asks himself: "React? But how?"[17] His answer takes the form of a historical vignette: "A fine story . . . the Great Age of the Arverni."

> Attacked by the Romans, Bituit, king of the barbarian Gauls, called together all his warriors. . . . He advanced on his silver-plated chariot with bronze axles, wearing a bronze helmet and adorned with golden necklaces and bracelets. His pack of hunting dogs accompanied him. Behind the squadrons of his escort came two hundred thousand Gauls with their long, double-edged swords, their pikes with sparkling iron points, and their great flat shields of wicker or wood, painted in bright colors. When from the top of the hills the king saw below, in the valley of the Rhone, the little square of the Roman legions, he exclaimed: "There will hardly be enough today for my dogs to pick over."

The message is clear: against the Jews, those new invaders, the hunting pack of "our ancestors the Gauls" has to be revived.[18] Anti-Semitism thus returns to the theme of the war between races developed by nineteenth-century French historiography, but immediately gives it the form of a manhunt of a heroic type.

In reality, of course, there was nothing glorious about the persecutions. Neither silver plating nor gold ornaments. Bernard Goldstein, who was later one of the organizers of the insurrection in the Warsaw Ghetto, tells what the beginning of a pogrom looked like in Poland in 1940: "Groups of hooligans, mostly youths, stormed through the Jewish sections of Warsaw. They charged down the streets shouting, 'Beat the Jews! Kill the Jews!' They broke into Jewish homes and stores, smashed furniture, seized valuables, and beat the occupants."[19] To these hunts, the Jewish workers' movement opposed political self-defense: "Despite that danger, we concluded that we had no choice, we must strike back. . . . [W]e decided to fight back with 'cold weapons,' iron pipes and brass knuckles, but not with knives or firearms. . . . Every fighting contingent was mobilized: slaughterhouse workers, transport workers, party members. . . . When the pogromists appeared in these sections on the following morning they were surprised to find our comrades waiting for them. A bloody battle broke out immediately. Ambulances rushed to carry off wounded pogromists."[20]

For a petite bourgeoisie that lived in fear of racial degeneration, the hunting ideal appeared more generally to be a means of physical and moral regeneration. As a nineteenth-century publicist put it: "Ask a petit-bourgeois about the benefits of hunting; that direct heir of the proud Gauls, that depository of the best-established traditions of our distant ancestors will not fail to reply: Hunting increases the strength of our race."[21]

This theme was made into an anthropological theory by reactionary thinkers obsessed with the "decline of the West." They theorized the predatory nature of man the better to call for a reawakening of buried instincts. This anthropology of the predator was most explicitly developed in Germany, by Oswald Spengler. As Jacques Bouveresse reminds us, it was Karl Kraus who explained the political implications of this philosophy: by praising the ability to attack the weakest "with intelligent determination," by glorifying "the intoxication of the emotion felt when the knife slices into the enemy's body, when the smell of blood and the groans reach the triumphant senses," Spengler had in reality provided "the intellectual foundation for the processes that took place in Dachau and Sonnenberg, in the Hedemannstrasse and the Papestrasse."[22] He called for an endorsement of predatory violence. The Nazis found in this one of the bases of their political ideology: cruelty and implacable predation as an ideal of power. In fact, the regime's dignitaries, who imagined themselves to be blond hordes and beasts of prey, loved hunting parties. Göring was particularly proud of his nickname, the *Reichsjägermeister*, the great Huntsman of the Reich.

Anti-Semitic and xenophobic hunting had a power of social mobilization that the Nazis knew how to fuel and capture in order to make it the vector of its conquest of power. The coup d'état and the pack: that was their strategy.

But once the Nazis had seized power, hunting Jews was to lose its mob dimension and become a police activity. Thus, it was used twice, so to speak, in different forms: first as an instrument of dissolving mobilization against the former power of the state, and then as the central instrument in the exercise of state power. A transition from pack hunts to state hunts.

From this point of view, Kristallnacht marked in 1938 a transition from old forms to new ones: the ultimate staging of a

FIGURE 8. "Man, the hunter": Hermann Göring in hunting attire. "Hermann Göring als Privatmann bei der Jagd," Dokumentationsarchiv des Österreichischen Widerstandes, inventory number 9782.

pogrom-hunt before the full deployment of state hunting. The hunt for Jews ceased to be disorganized and carried out by packs; it became planned, bureaucratic, and centralized. Then it could follow the old mottoes implacably, better than any bloodthirsty pack had ever been able to, with all the methodical coldness of state machinery. Already murderous, it now became genocidal.

Anti-Semitism, which had previously been reformulated in terms of biological racism, was now integrated as a political mechanism into the practice of state power. Foucault has shown how in a biopolitical context racism becomes an operator of power that makes it possible to draw, in a biological *continuum* of the population, a line between those who are to live and those who are to die.[23] Unlike religious identity, belonging to a race cannot be renounced: it is posited as substantial, and as a result it tends to imply the physical elimination of those who have been racified.

When associated with this apparatus, the accepted reference to hunting and to natural predatory relationships also made it possible to carry out another operation in order to provide a foundation for racist violence. Hitler had noted, in private: "Many Jews have not become aware of the destructive nature of their existence. But anyone who destroys life exposes himself to death, and no exception will be made for them! Who is to blame when the cat eats the mouse?"[24] The underlying idea was that a predator is never to blame for his violence, because hunting is part of his vital nature, as being hunted is part of the vital nature of his prey. It is not by virtue of an initial aggression, a kind of legitimate defense, that the cat is justified in attacking the mouse. On the contrary, as Hitler concedes, no mouse may ever have harmed a cat. But it doesn't matter, because thinking that way would be once again to situate oneself in the old framework of the law of war, in which the riposte is the central concept. But with biopolitical racism, we are no longer situated in this kind of rationality. The right to kill is not based on what the other has done, but on what he is and on what we are, and on the necessary order of this relationship. The violence of the racist state is not an act of reprisal; it has nothing to do with a law of war: it depends on a completely different rationality—that of hunting and natural predation. The hostility between predator and prey does not have to be founded on a right of aggression that determines the legitimate cases, because it is inscribed as a necessity in the nature of the species or races involved. By setting up animal hunting as the model of legitimacy for its violence, state racism (contrary to a whole side of the modern philosophical tradition) reduces political law to a zoological definition of natural law—in which law has no limits other than those of power, and of a power biologically defined. The model of zoological predation thus makes it possible to naturalize the right to kill, to make of it a state prerogative based on racial superiority. The "right" to engage in genocide is thus situated in the continuity of a natural relationship between prey and predator. The cynegetic model serves as a normative reference point for the racist state by including murderous violence in the necessary order of vital violence.

In February 1945, some prisoners of war escaped from the Mauthausen concentration camp. The Nazi authorities launched a vast operation that lasted several days, known under the name *Mühlviertler Hasenjagd*—"Hare hunt in the Mühlviertel." In this manhunt, not only the army, the SS, and the police force, but also the local civilian population took part. A hybrid form of state and popular hunting. As if, through this final mobilization of the population in the hunt, the moribund Nazi state apparatus had wanted to cede back to the pack its cynegetic prerogatives during a last common hunting battue.

CHAPTER 12

Hunting Illegals

Behold, thou hast driven me this day away from the ground; and
from thy face I shall be hidden; and I shall be a fugitive and a
wanderer on the earth, and whoever finds me will slay me.
GENESIS 4:14–15

He . . . tried to escape, apparently fearing that his location might be
discovered. An officer with the anti-criminality brigade set out in
pursuit of him. Then he threw himself into the water, from which he
was shortly afterward fished out in a critical condition. He died at the
hospital as a result of cardiac arrest.
"DEATH OF AN ILLEGAL IMMIGRANT WHO TRIED TO
ESCAPE THE POLICE," *REUTERS*, 4 APRIL 2008[1]

IN GENESIS, Cain is doomed to wander the Earth. This exile
makes him a universal prey: "Whoever finds me will slay me."
To remedy this dangerous vulnerability, God marks him with
a protective sign: "The Lord put a mark on Cain, lest any who
came upon him should kill him."[2] What was this sign? The text
does not tell us, and interpretations differ. For some commen-
tators, it was nothing other than the fear that agitated Cain's
body, "the trembling of his members that made him different
and stand out."[3] But whatever it was, this mark was of transcen-
dental origin.

What protection can those who are expelled from the protective order enjoy? Transposed to the civil and political sphere in societies in which protection has been monopolized by the authorities of the nation-state, the question becomes particularly acute for those who are excluded from it, in view of the fact that in terrestrial politics, there are no marks of transcendent protection, no divine safe-conducts.

This is the problem Hannah Arendt raised with regard to stateless people, in whom she saw a "modern expulsion from humanity" with "much more radical consequences than the ancient and medieval custom of outlawry."[4] Arendt knew that the ancient forms of banishment—which she correctly analyzed as a "substitute for a police force, designed to compel criminals to surrender"[5]—put the life of the exile at the mercy of anyone he encountered. But she maintained that the modern exclusion of stateless people was still more radical. To understand in what way, we have to examine the specific characteristics of this new form of proscription.

The legal exclusion of stateless people is no longer presented as punishment for a crime, but as a *status*, directly connected with the individuals' political status. If the stateless person is excluded from the system of legal protection, that is not because he has *committed* an infraction: on the contrary, he *is* himself that infraction, by the simple fact of existing, by his sole presence on the territory of the nation-state. Making persons infractions, making their lives a permanent infraction, is thus the first characteristic of this new system of legal exclusion.[6]

This new form of proscription is no longer so much an expedient testifying to the weakness of the sovereign power as, on the contrary, the basis for an indefinite inflation of a police power exercised on subjects deprived of legal protection.[7]

In the context of a humanity organized into nation-states, the exclusion of stateless people is no longer equivalent to the loss of this or that system of national protection but to the loss of any possible protection. Because of the practical identification of the rights of man with the rights of citizens, and of the latter with the rights of those having a certain nationality, their guarantee by the state is conditional on the admission of individuals into the sphere of nationality. What they lose when they lose nationality is, thus, not only specific rights but even the right to have rights: "Only with a completely organized humanity could the loss of home and political status become identical with expulsion from humanity altogether."[8] The paradox is that what has been called "the rights of Man" has been so much identified with the rights of nationals that as soon as Men are presented qua Men, these rights can no longer be accorded them: "The paradox involved in the loss of human rights is that such loss coincides with the instant when a person becomes a human being in general."[9]

Modern proscription is both more subtle and more methodical than the earlier one. Above all, it is carried out through administrative procedures. Its mechanics is bureaucratic and its instruments consist of paper. Modern states have concentrated in their hands the monopoly on the means of certifying personal existence. One becomes an illegal by not having papers, official documents that can be presented to anyone who asks for them. As Arendt noted, "society has discovered discrimination as the great social weapon by which one may kill men without any bloodshed; . . . passports or birth certificates, and sometimes even income tax receipts, are no longer formal papers but matters of social distinction."[10] Being illegal means not having papers in a context in which a paper identity has become one of the essential modes of the legal subject's existence, not only in his relationship to the state, but also for all the transactions that constitute the fabric of his daily life.

The problem Arendt formulated regarding stateless persons persists today for migrants without papers, whose status combines the preceding four characteristics: criminalization of existence, inflation of police control, exclusion from human rights, and paper death.

This new form of legal proscription, which is distinct from that of stateless persons, is a recent historical product of policies of the *illegalization* of migrants, whose progress can be followed law by law, measure by measure, in most northern hemisphere states since the early 1970s.[11] This new situation of the illegality of immigrant workers is connected with states' refusal to grant them the right to reside and work legally. At the same time that the conditions for entrance and residence have been made more restrictive, they have thrown an increasing number of workers into illegality.

On the old and still active demarcation according to nationality has now been superposed a new line of exclusion formulated in the name of a principle of territoriality. In France, even though social rights tend to be granted to all residents without regard to nationality, the authorities have gradually introduced a new criterion of discrimination, that of the legality of the residence.[12] It is an example of the creation of a crime sui generis, for the purpose of legal exclusion of migrants, who are supposed thereby to be dissuaded from entering a territory that refuses them access to basic rights.

However, even if they are considered to be there illegally, migrants are in fact on the territory; they reside there physically and socially. So that the primary effect of this legal exclusion is not to make them disappear, but to withhold a whole series of rights from them. Thus we arrive at the paradox that the chief effect of these measures legally excluding migrants without papers, even though decreed in the name of territorial sovereignty, is to produce situations on the territory in which the law no longer applies, in the form of enclaves or autonomous zones attached to individuals who have become, in a way, extraterritorials. This situation causes a rupture with respect to the old principle of territorial sovereignty that maintains that everything that is *on* the territory *belongs to* the territory,[13] given that residing on the territory no longer suffices to be completely subject, de facto, to the law that applies to it. Excluding these residents from the law is tantamount to a suspension of the law, a suspension that derives from the legislation itself. Thus, on the pretext of enforcing a territorial borderline, we have created on the territory a legal borderline between those who can be protected by the law and those who cannot.

Considered nonexistent even though they exist, these individuals are denied the legal recognition of their actual social integration. Like those of the persons who are physically alive but legally dead, the relationships they form can only remain informal. Here we find another characteristic trait of the status of the illegal alien: the prohibition on helping him. This is the "crime of solidarity": "Any person who, by direct or indirect assistance, facilitates or attempts to facilitate the illegal entry, travel, or residence of a foreigner in France shall be punished by five years' imprisonment and a fine of 30,000 Euros."[14] In addition to criminalizing private solidarity, legal exclusion also extends to the benefits of the welfare state. In France, in recent years, the authorities have made repeated attempts to restrict the state medical assistance on which people without papers depend for their access to medical care. Without mentioning the budgetary aspect of the question, in practice "the intensification of police action to arrest people without papers leads them to stop taking steps to obtain state medical aid. They no longer claim their rights, for fear that doing so will lead to their arrest."[15] So in general, as Amnesty International explains, "The fact that they have no legal status means that they are often reluctant or unable to demand their rights with regard to work or other human rights."[16]

Proposition 187, passed in California in 1994, made explicit the philosophical principles that underlie such policies of exclusion from fundamental rights. In order to justify the exclusion of illegal aliens from social services, from healthcare and education, the preamble to this proposition invoked the citizens' right to protection—reinterpreted as a right to protection "from any person or persons entering this country unlawfully."[17] Here we find once again the nationalistic restriction of the concept of protection, which, as we have seen, has constituted the programmatic basis of political xenophobia since the middle of the nineteenth century.

Access to unconditional rights has thus been made conditional on the state's arbitrary definition of the legal character of residency. Hannah Arendt's warning must be taken seriously: the nation-state's restriction of access to human rights inevitably produces lethal phenomena of exclusion.

However, illegalization does not function simply as a measure of exclusion. As Nicholas De Genova emphasizes, at the same time it also has a paradoxical function of inclusion. Legal exclusion corresponds to an "active process of inclusion through illegalization,"[18] chiefly in the sense that the legal exclusion of workers without papers makes possible their employment under conditions of extreme vulnerability. Excluded from legality, they find themselves included in particularly intensive forms of exploitation. "Once we recognize that undocumented migrations are constituted in order not to physically exclude them but instead, to socially include them under imposed conditions of enforced and protracted vulnerability, it is not difficult to fathom how migrants' endurance of many years of 'illegality' can serve as a disciplinary apprenticeship in the subordination of their labor."[19] Vulnerability through legal exclusion serves as a disciplinary antechamber, a way of rendering people docile by making them insecure.

Analyzing the functioning of the contemporary power of illegalization thus requires us to pay attention to what Judith Butler calls "complex modes of governmentality in ways that are not easily reducible to sovereign acts."[20] Contrary to what the term used to designate them suggests, legally dispossessed people today are not solely "without": they are not completely defined by their lack of something. Excluded from legal forms of membership, disqualified for citizenship, they are at the same time actively "qualified" for illegal life. Far from returning to a prepolitical condition of a biological order, their lives are actively produced and socially saturated by power. Specifically criticizing Agamben's thesis, Butler emphasizes that modern illegals are not "undifferentiated instances of 'bare life' but highly juridified states of dispossession."[21]

But what kind of life does one live when life is denied by the state? In *The Holy Family*, Marx mocks the idea that the state's nonrecognition of a social phenomenon is equivalent to its real disappearance. This way of seeing things, related for example to the religious question, would consist in thinking that no longer including holidays in the law would be equivalent to declaring "that Christianity has ceased to exist." To this thesis of the performativity of legal discourse Marx opposes a realist conception of the mode of social phenomena's existence in their relation to state recognition: "in the developed modern state . . . this proclamation of their civil death corresponds to their most vigorous life, which henceforth obeys its own laws undisturbed and develops to its full scope."[22] The state's nonrecognition of a phenomenon does not make it disappear but rather frees it from the straitjacket of the law and returns it to the most primitive forms of its social life. Its legal death is the beginning of its "anarchical" life. Similarly, a subject deprived of legal existence does not return to a biological, presocial life, but to a social life without the law of civil society, that is, first of all, to an unrestrained exploitation. For migrant workers, the primary effect of their illegalization is the deregulation of the wage relationship. Social relationships that are formed without a code, without a guarantee, and almost without recourse. Today, illegalization no longer exposes people "to the beasts of the forest, the birds of the sky, and the fish that live under the waters," as in ancient formulas of banishment, but to the predation of a labor market in which, more than ever, workers who put their bodies on the market can expect only one thing: to be skinned.

Market predation and sovereign exclusion develop close relations of complementarity. Economic predation on the labor market takes place, in fact, against the background not only of legal exclusion but also of police searches preliminary to expulsion. It is precisely this insecurity with regard to the law and the police, organized with a view to expulsion, that also leads, as a secondary effect, to the production of a workforce that is all the easier to exploit economically the more it is made vulnerable by the state. Hunts to expel, police and governmental hunts, are associated with predatory mechanisms for procuring and exploiting an unofficial workforce. Police hunts and market predation are connected with each other: hunts to expel and hunts to acquire.

Manhunting is a technique of governing by making people feel insecure—putting people on edge, against the background of living in constant danger of being tracked down and deported. These effects are part of a deliberate and conscious strategy. The agents of the hunt willingly recognize this. Thus a lieutenant-colonel in the French national police, in an interview in which he also did not hesitate to use the term *roundups* (*rafles*), said: "In fact, I try to put foreigners who are in an irregular situation in a climate of insecurity. They have to know that we can check their papers at any time. They have to fear that."[23] Echoing his statement, defenders of illegal aliens make a similar observation: "Living in the shadows, without rights or in hiding, means living in permanent fear of denunciation and extortion, because if one's situation is discovered, the punishment incurred will be detention or immediate expulsion. It means feeling a total absence of protection and recourse with regard to the administration, bosses, and owners, as well as with regard to illness, accidents, and disputes. It means fearing any kind of social contact. . . . It means having to be constantly on your guard."[24]

If we can speak of hunting illegal aliens, that is because today expulsions no longer depend on random checks for papers. Under pressure from xenophobic politicians, quotas now have to be filled. But filling quotas implies a policy of proactive pursuit. As Emmanuel Terray explains, "Technically speaking, when you want to arrest undesirables, you have to go find them. The fact that in this area the French police have been given numerical targets, and are held responsible by their superiors for meeting them, results in this hunt taking entirely spectacular forms."[25] Thus, one police officer also says, regarding this reorientation, "Before, bringing in a foreigner who didn't have the necessary papers was a shame, a waste of time. Now they do practically nothing else."[26]

To fill its arrest quotas, the police uses a certain number of techniques. In his *Manual of Ethnography*, Marcel Mauss indicates that "hunting can be studied in two main ways: according to the weapon used, and according to the game hunted."[27] Let us first examine the weapons.

The first of these weapons is the identity check. This is a filtering technique that calls for establishing a checkpoint where people pass by, preferably where the individuals sought live. For illegal aliens in Paris, as a police officer again explains, "It's easy. You go to Belleville, and you're sure to find some and meet the quotas."[28] Then a "file check" is carried out in order to identify "those who can be arrested." The EURODAC database, a system for recognizing fingerprints, today inventories more than a million illegal aliens and asylum seekers. For a long time, until the first third of the nineteenth century, the state branded its convicts to make them identifiable in the event that they escaped or committed further crimes. Today, in the system of biometric identification, no mark needs to be put on people, because the mark is the body itself. In Calais, however, the refugees have invented a technique for defeating biometric checks: "A fire is kept continually burning. It serves to heat water (for tea, laundry, and personal hygiene), but also to heat iron bars that the migrants use to mutilate the tips of their fingers to efface their fingerprints."[29]

When an individual who is being checked runs away, a pursuit follows:

> I was bumped into by a young man who looked like a teenager; he ran away like a madman. I heard a voice shouting, "Stop him! Police!!! Stop him." . . . I saw the young man take off down the avenue with the two policeman running after him. I said to myself that

when one is being chased, one finds in one's body all the energy to go fast, one can't be caught, and yet the policemen were making their best effort. . . . I wondered what he had done—attacked someone, dealt drugs? The young man turned left before the bridge. The exhausted policemen slowed down. . . . I slowed down, I too looked, I didn't see anything. I said to myself that if the young man was in the water, I would see him; he hadn't had time to swim across the arm of the river. . . . Then I continued on my way, saying to myself that he had succeeded in escaping. That evening, I read on the Net: "Death of an illegal alien pursued by the police."[30]

The technique of ambushing consists in setting up at a promising site and waiting:

In 2007, taking advantage of free meals being distributed by the Restos du Coeur on the Place de la République in Paris, about twenty illegal aliens were arrested. . . . "It's like for animals: the bait in the center, the hunters lying in ambush, trucks to haul off the captured." Wednesday, the same game in Rouen. Set up for hardly a quarter of an hour on the Place des Emmurés, the volunteers from Camions du Coeur saw the police arrive just as they were preparing to serve meals, to hand out hygienic products and protection against the cold. The result: a dozen illegals arrested.[31]

Areas around schools are another place where arrests are easy to make. In Paris, on 20 March 2007, Xiangxig Chen came, as he did every day, to pick up his four-year-old grandson at the preschool in the rue Rampal. Police officers were waiting there. The grandfather was arrested in a bar down the street. Parents belonging to the RESF network sounded the alarm: "A crowd is forming in front of the bistro. 'You're going to understand very soon why you have to get out of here,' a police officer shouts at them. He opens the door of his vehicle and out come two muzzled dogs that he unleashes on the crowd. . . . The policemen get out their batons and shoot tear gas at the crowd just as the children are coming out into the street."[32]

When a combing or police raid ends with the arrest of a large group, it is called a "roundup" (*rafle*). In its report for 2006, La Cimade drew up a list of the roundups of illegal aliens carried out by the French police in the course of the year.[33] This term, as Emmanuel Blanchard tells us, designates a precise police technique, namely, according to a definition known at least since 1829, "massive arrests made without warning by the police in a suspect place."[34] A historical and political remark: using this word does not imply the amalgamation of contemporary state xenophobia with the state-sponsored racial extermination of the 1940s.[35] Even if they turn out to be lethal, contemporary roundups/expulsions are not ordered with genocidal objectives in mind. If we have to find predecessors for them, they can, however, be connected with the practice of hunting down "undesirables" that flourished during the interwar period, at the same time that a menacing far right was growing in power and legislation against foreigners was being hardened. At that time, newspapers described roundups and manhunts in French cities, and even provided illustrations of them.

The roundups might also be connected with earlier *rondes-battues*, which consisted in closing off a perimeter and then checking and arresting those who were caught within it. In Calais, when the "jungle" was evacuated, the hunt led to arrests on a huge scale that ended with the following scene: "The migrants file by, their eyes red, hanging their heads as if ashamed, surrounded by men in blue who are carrying out a triage—that's their term—between minors and adults before leading them to the buses that are to take them to police headquarters."[36]

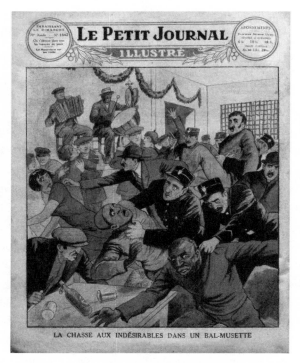

FIGURE 9. Hunting undesirables in a dance hall. *Le Petit-journal illustrée*, no. 1842 (1927).

Distinct from roundups, the practice of arrests at home has developed in recent years, again under the pressure of numerical quotas. In Amiens, on 9 August 2007, the police bangs on the door of an illegal alien couple from Chechnya. The family attempts to escape. Their son, Ivan Dembsky, twelve years old, tries to cross over to the neighbor's balcony. He falls from the fourth floor. He slips into a coma and dies at the hospital.[37] The prime minister issues a communiqué in which he "expresses all his compassion to the parents" for this "accidental fall," while insisting that "the immigration policy the nation wants . . . requires firmness and a strong commitment on the part of all agents of the state."[38]

In addition to combings, raids, roundups, and arrests at home, the state also sets traps. In this case, the procedure consists in encouraging illegal aliens to come to the prefectures on the pretext of a personal examination of their applications for regular papers. In February 2008, the prefecture in Nanterre composed a circular addressed to its agents, explaining that "foreigners applying for regularization must no longer send their files by mail but present themselves physically." When they were asked to come to the window in person, it was so they could be arrested there. The circular then explained how the operation was to be carried out: "The following chronological schema is applied: The foreigner hands over his passport to the agent. The foreigner is asked to take a seat in the waiting room. The agent refers the matter to the head of the deportation department (in his absence: the head of the bureau or his assistant). The department head refers the matter to the DDSP and informs the head of the reception department. The arrest will be made in a closed booth."[39]

"On principle, I detest manhunts. . . . I think that if manhunts are deplorable, hunting sons is even more deplorable"—it is Éric Besson who is speaking here.[40] But all sons, of course, do not deserve the same empathy: everything depends on who their father is. The "manhunt" to which the minister of immigration and national identity was referring was the outcry aroused by the appointment of President Sarkozy's son to head the development council (EPAD) of the department of Hauts-de-Seine. Morality and the capacity for indignation, just like "principles," have variable geometries. This kind of dissymmetry is characteristic of the double moral standard of the dominant: deploring the very metaphorical hunting of the sons of the powerful when one is oneself organizing a very literal hunt for the children of the most disadvantaged.[41] Beyond the anecdote, what is manifested here is, very profoundly, the duplicity of the normative system that is being set up on both sides of the internal borderline between national identity, on the one hand, and the legality of residence, on the other, a borderline between those who are accorded an inalienable right to protection, and those to whom all protection, even the most basic, is denied. Between those who can be hunted and those who cannot, even if only in discourse. Between the "protected" and the rest.

CONCLUSION

A MAN IS RUNNING. Armed pursuers are chasing him. The scene has been repeated ever since a barbarian was caught at the gates of an ancient city, right down to that shadowy figure disappearing down the corridor in a Parisian metro station. Beneath the apparent similarity of the situations are concealed, however, very different forms of power.

There are cynegetic powers, ones that are exercised by tracking and capturing their subjects. This book outlines the history of their changing morphology. Whereas an author like René Girard postulates a kind of invariant of violence in human societies that is for him essentially based on a logic of expiatory sacrifice, I have instead tried to bring out what was specific, in their motives and functions, to each of the great historical phenomena of manhunting. Contrary to what the theory of the scapegoat claims, the choice of prey, for example, is never arbitrary or "relatively indifferent":[1] it is governed by targeted strategies that remain unintelligible so long as they are reduced to the uniform model of a sacrificial violence.

Cynegetic power appears first of all as the condition for ancient slave-owning domination. A power of capturing to provide a supply of slave labor, a technique of violent acquisition at the root of the master's economic power, these Greek hunts were authorized by an ontological division of humanity into masters and slaves by nature. With the biblical tradition, a second conception of cynegetic power emerges: the figure of Nimrod, the hunter-king capturing his subjects by violence, is opposed point for point to pastoral power, of which it constitutes the symmetrical double: immanence versus transcendence, territorial accumulation versus gregarious mobility, predation versus benevolence, massification versus individualization—everything separates these two models of political sovereignty. Although it is defined by opposition to hunting sovereignty, pastoralism produces within itself specific forms of predation that are paradoxically founded on an imperative of protection: it is no longer a question of acquiring subjects by violence, but of eliminating diseased members of the flock, subjects that are excluded from the community in the name of the latter's preservation. This model of hunts to exclude is continued in the practice of sovereign power with the penal exclusion of criminals and hunts for wolf-men carried out in the form of popular battues.

These are the three great forms of cynegetic power that were available and conceivable on the threshold of modernity. However, one event was to upset everything. To the rise of Western capitalism corresponds, on three continents, the outbreak of new manhunts. In the Americas, it is the hunt for Indians, the hunt to enslave and the hunt to kill, justified theoretically both as a hunt for slaves by nature and as a hunt for those banned from humanity, in a schema in which the ancient categories merge in order to produce a new theory of conquest. On the African continent, the delegation of hunting to local intermediaries was accompanied by a paradoxical theory of the Africans' responsibility for the slave trade in which, on a racist basis, the prey, which are said to hunt each other, come to bear the historical blame for their own enslavement. At the same time, on the old

Continent, vast hunts for the poor occur along with the formation of a wage-earning class and the rise of an increasing police
power whose tracking and hunting operations are henceforth
linked in an essential way with apparatuses of confinement.

These new kinds of manhunts were the spectacular manifestations of what Marx called the phase of the primitive accumulation of capital. The great hunting power, which casts its nets
on a scale unprecedented in the history of humanity, is that of
capital.

In the metropolitan space, the state, breaking with the old
model of banishment, now monopolizes the power of legitimate
hunting. However, phenomena of popular hunting reappear
within it, in the form of disturbing hunting packs that are mobilized against the background of racial caste domination (lynching), putting groups in competition on the market for wage
labor (hunts for foreigners), and the redirection of political
antagonisms (hunts for Jews). Extreme right-wing movements
recognize in the hunting pack a social force capable of providing
them with a base for their political hegemony. Having come to
power, they institute a state racism in which racist hunting becomes the heart of a program whose murderous goals can then
be pursued with the means of state power. The zoological model
of natural predation is associated with the biopolitical mechanisms of state racism to provide the matrix for legitimizing the
genocidal project.

Today, state xenophobia, if it breaks with biological racism's hunts to exterminate, reactivates and reconfigures certain
fundamental traits of the ancient hunts of proscription. The policies of illegalizing migrants are paradoxically based on a territorial conception of sovereignty that its practice in fact ends up
denying. A murderous policy which, through legal exclusion,

ensures the paradoxical inclusion of these new dispossessed by law into relationships of exploitation at the same time that it makes them vulnerable through active policies of tracking them and making them feel insecure.

The history of a power is also that of struggles. How can people free themselves from a relationship of hunting and predation? How, from the position of a prey, can a political subjectivity be formed?

The first difficulty has to do with the identification of prey as being essentially *victims*. I have tried to show how this kind of political identification bore within itself a dilemma, the dilemma of the victim, in which the subjects find themselves confronted by a false choice between the recognition of their status as victims at the price of negating their power to act and the recognition of their power to act at the price of negating the guilt of their tormentors. This antinomy, which constitutes a powerful political trap, is based on the false idea that the historical responsibility for their enslavement has to be attributed to the oppressed in order for the task of their emancipation to become their own. Moving out of this rut involves reactivating nonjudicial categories of political identification and the recognition of a subjectivity that is active because it is already engaged in a process of self-emancipation.

Manhunting involves a specific relationship between consciousnesses whose peculiar dialectic I have sought to trace: a dialectic of the hunter and the hunted whose elements differ from those of the classical schema of Hegelian phenomenology. Caught from the outset in a dissymmetrical power relationship, the prey can move beyond its initial state of radical concern and constitute an active subjectivity through the paradoxical internalization of the position of objectivity that is assigned him by the hunter's perspective. A reversal then occurs in which the former prey becomes a hunter in turn. But at the same time an aporia appears, that of the simple reversion or nondialectical reversal of the relationship of predation, in which the positions are simply inverted, whereas the fundamental relationship remains intact. That is the tragic irony of the prey who escapes only by becoming what it sought to escape from. Moving out of this rut presupposes the formulation of a critical theory of political violence.

The other great obstacle to the constitution of a political subjectivity in the system of cynegetic power is the impasse of the internal reproduction of the relationship of predation. When no other option appears to be available, in order to cease to be a prey, than to become a hunter in turn, dynamics of interpredation develop that echo and duplicate ad infinitum in dominated subgroups the principal relationship of predation. This is the fundamental strategic problem of the division and dispersal of the prey collective.

This problem arises in a particularly acute form in a context in which political xenophobia has instrumentalized the phenomena of the hunting pack and of putting people in competition with one another in order to make them the basis for a program of racial exclusion. The principal operation of xenophobic politics consists in taking into account the powerful social demand for protection by retranslating it in the restrictive mode of a sharp division between those who must be protected and those who cannot be protected—or worse yet, who must not be protected because it is in fact from them that other people have to be protected. The identification of the sphere of legitimate protection with the autochthonous group, whether in the biopolitical modality of race, the historical-cultural modality of national identity, or the administrative and political modality of legal residence, leads necessarily to the creation of abandoned populations who are exposed, without any protection, to predatory relationships. This type of exclusion is all the more efficient, and all the more productive of deleterious effects, as the functions of protection have been centralized by the institution that has both drawn the borderlines of the group of humans that are to be protected and has the means to hunt down those whom it has excluded from its definition.

The study of predatory relationships among humans and their political history raises in a central way the problem of *protection*. If withdrawing the protection of the law produces prey, it also gives us, by contrast, an essential clue to what should be the vocation of a universal political community, its *telos*: providing collective protection against interhuman predatory relationships.

POSTSCRIPT

As I am completing the writing of this book, I read in the press:

> In Italy, the hunt for immigrants in Rosarno. Migrants, seasonal workers, forced to engage in an exodus after having been subjected to a genuine manhunt.
>
> It all began Thursday evening, when young Calabrians with rifles fired on migrants. The outcome: two wounded. In protest, the migrants burned a few trash cans and numerous cars. Friday, two thousand immigrant workers took part in a demonstration to protest against the vexations and attacks to which they are subjected. "The Italians here are racists!" read the signs they carried. Four thousand seasonal migrants come every winter to work in the citrus orchards from dawn to dusk for twenty-five Euros a day and crowd into a slum on the edge of town. In the evening, attacks against migrants flared again, more violent than ever. Part of the local population, two to three hundred persons, carried on a reign of terror using iron bars, rifles, and barricades, and besieging even the headquarters of a migrants' association. The climate established by Silvio Berlusconi's government, with its ministers issuing rival declarations against "clandestine workers," was not unrelated to the fear felt by some of the inhabitants of Rosarno.[1]

NOTES

INTRODUCTION

1. Letter from Robert Gaguin, quoted in Philippe de Commines, *Lettres et négociations de Philippe de Commines* (Brussels: Devaux, 1867), vol. 1, p. 335

2. *Dictionnaire de l'Académie française*, vol. 1 (Paris: Guillaume, 1831), p. 227.

3. Honoré de Balzac, *La Comédie humaine. Études de moeurs. Scènes de la vie politique*, vol. 12 (Paris: Furne, 1846), p. 299; *An Historical Mystery* (Boston: Roberts Brothers, 1891), p. 137.

4. Hannah Arendt, *The Origins of Totalitarianism* (New York: Harcourt, 1966), p. 457.

CHAPTER 1
The Hunt for Bipedal Cattle

1. Thucydides, *History of the Peloponnesian War* 6, trans. R. Warner (London: Penguin, 1954), p. 449.

2. Plato, *Sophist* 222c, in E. Hamilton and H. Cairns, eds., *The Collected Dialogues of Plato* (Princeton, NJ: Princeton University Press, 1961), p. 964.

3. Plato, *Laws* 823e, trans. B. Jowett, in Hamilton and Cairns, *The Collected Dialogues of Plato*, p. 1393.

4. Aristotle, *Politics* 1256b, in Roger S. Bagnall and Peter Derow, *The Hellenistic Period: Historical Sources in Translation* (Oxford: Blackwell, 2004), p. 1137.

5. In the *Sophist*, Plato distinguishes between two main kinds of technologies: the productive arts, which create their object, and the arts of acquisition, which do not fabricate their object but instead appropriate existing things.

6. See Henry Joly's commentary on the *Crito* in his *Études platoniciennes: La question des étrangers* (Paris: Vrin, 1992), p. 16.

7. See Richard Bodeis, "Les considérations aristotéliciennes sur la brutalité" in B. Cassin and J.-L. Labarrière, *L'Animal dans l'antiquité* (Paris: Vrin, 1997), pp. 247–258, 254.

8. Aristotle, *Politics* 1254b, p. 1133.

9. Plato, *Laws* 6.777b, p. 1353.

10. Plutarch, *Life of Lycurgus* 28.3–7.

11. Jean Ducat, "Le Mépris des Hilotes," *Annales* 29 (1974): 1456–1459.

12. Thucydides, *History of the Peloponnesian War* 6, p. 313.

CHAPTER 2

Nimrod, or Cynegetic Sovereignty

1. Genesis 10:8–9.

2. *Sepher Ha-Zohar, Le livre de la splendeur. Commentaire sur Deutéronome* (Paris: Maisonneuve et Larose, 1985), vol. 6, p. 182.

3. Friedrich Julius Wilhelm Schroeder, *Premier livre de Moïse— Commentaire* (Paris: Ducloux, 1850), vol. 1, p. 282.

4. An unproven etymology derives *Nimrod* from the Hebrew מרד, *mārad*, "to rebel," with the ambiguity that in this form the word would rather signify, in the passive, the person against whom the rebellion takes place. Nimrod appears both as the one who disobeys and the one who elicits disobedience.

5. Jean Bodin, *Six Books of the Commonwealth* (Oxford: Blackwell, 1955), p. 57.

6. In these theories, the immanence of consent will be opposed to the immanence of force. The theme emerges during the English Civil War of 1640–1650. The revolutionary movement of the Levellers, which represented a radical egalitarianism, used the theory of conquest and biblical genealogy to challenge the foundations of sovereign authority and to oppose to it the free agreement of subjects with natural rights. When in 1649 John Lilburne, "Freeborn John," one of the greatest of the Leveller pamphleteers, attacked Oliver Cromwell's absolute power, he quite naturally compared Cromwell to "that great and mighty hunter, Nimrod." See David Loewenstein, *Representing Revolution in Milton and His Contemporaries* (Cambridge: Cambridge University Press, 2001), p. 43. Similarly, much later, when Rousseau raises in his *Émile* the question of whether force can ever form a permanent law, he refers explicitly to "the force of King Nimrod, who, it is said, subjected the

first peoples to it." J.-J. Rousseau, *Œuvres complètes* (Paris: Gallimard, 1959), vol. 4, p. 837.

7. René François Rohrbacher, *Histoire universelle de l'Église Catholique* (Paris: Gaume, 1857), vol. 1, p. 312.

8. Michel Foucault, *Security, Territory, Population* (London: Palgrave Macmillan, 2007), p. 170.

9. Hegel, commenting on Josephus (*Antiquities of the Jews*, book 1, chap. 4, sect. 2) makes Nimrod the figure of the immanence of force, opposing him to the obedient Noah: "He defended himself against water by walls; he was a hunter and a king. In this battle against need, therefore, the elements, animals, and men had to endure the law of the stronger, though the law of a living being. Against the hostile power [of nature] Noah saved himself by subjecting both it and himself to something more powerful; Nimrod, by taming it himself." G. W. F. Hegel, *On Christianity: Early Theological Writings*, trans. T. M. Knox (Gloucester, MA: Peter Smith, 1970), p. 184.

10. The *Zohar* says that Nimrod's clothes came from Adam: "They had fallen into the hands of Nimrod; and it was thanks to these clothes that Nimrod was a great hunter." By Adam's clothes "the Zohar means the laws of nature, or physics, as we now say, which God revealed to Adam. It is certain . . . that according to the Zohar, Nimrod, having explained all phenomena on the basis of natural laws, led the people to believe that it is these laws that rule sovereignly over the world." *Sepher Ha-Zohar*, p. 101.

11. See Philippe Buc, "Pouvoir royal et commentaire de la Bible (1150–1350)," *Annales* 44 (1989): 691–713, 698.

12. Claude Thomasset, *Commentaire du Dialogue de Placides et Timeo* (Geneva: Droz, 1982), p. 217.

13. Quoted in Pierre Briant, "Chasses royales macédoniennes et chasses royales perses: Le thème de la chasse au lion sur la *Chasse de Vergina*," in Pierre Lévêque, *Dialogues d'histoire ancienne* (Besançon: PUFC, 1991), pp. 211–256, 219.

14. Matthew 4:18–20; Mark 1:17.

15. Thomas Hobbes, *Leviathan*, part 3, chap. 42.

16. If Nimrod serves at first to distinguish between the forms of religious power and the forms of political power, the topos of the hunter-king also developed as a weapon for criticizing monarchical authority. In the Middle Ages, the good shepherd-king is opposed to the bad hunter-king. In Renaissance humanism, the latter becomes the figure of the "demovore king," who has become, "instead of the shep-

herd of the people, a devourer of the people." Guillaume de Salluste Du Bartas, *La Seconde Semaine* (Paris: S.T.F.M., 1992), vol. 2, p. 313. In the struggles within Christianity, the theme of Nimrod was adopted by antipapist groups and turned against the ecclesiastical hierarchy, notably by Martin Luther.

17. See Foucault, *Security, Territory, Population*, p. 175.

CHAPTER 3
Diseased Sheep and Wolf-Men

1. Cited in Étienne-Léon de La Mothe-Langon, *Histoire de l'Inquisition en France* (Paris: Dentu, 1829), vol. 3, p. 210.

2. Bellarmine, *De pontif. Rom.*, book 5, chap. 7, quoted in *Abrégé de l'histoire des papes, depuis St. Pierre jusqu'à Clément XII* (N.p.: n.p., 1739), p. 181.

3. St Jerome, *ad Gal.* 5.

4. Brian P. Levack, *The Witch-hunt in Early Modern Europe* (London: Longman, 1987), p. 2.

5. Jacques Eveillon, *Traité des excommunications et monitoires* (Paris: Couterot, 1672), p. 28.

6. St. Thomas Aquinas, II, II, quaestio 11, art. 3, p. 360.

7. Albert Du Boys, *Histoire du droit criminel des peuples modernes* (Paris: Durand, 1854), pp. 122–124.

8. Robert Jacob, "Bannissement et rite de la langue tirée au Moyen Âge," *Annales* 55, no. 5 (2000): 1039–1079, 1043.

9. From Grimm on, the tendency in German historiography was to trace this motif back to the oldest German antiquity, but Jacoby showed that before the twelfth century the terms based on the root *warg* did not systematically refer to the wolf. See Michael Jacoby, *Wargus, vargr, Verbrecher, Wolf. Eine sprach-und rechtsgeschichtliche Untersuchung* (Uppsala: Almqvist & Wiksell, 1974).

10. Titre 38; see Julien Marie Le Huërou, *Histoire des institutions mérovingiennes*, vol. 1 (Paris: Joubert, 1843), p. 95.

11. See Jacob, "Bannissement et rite de la langue tirée au Moyen Âge," p. 1040.

12. On the basis of this text, historians of the law have constructed an interpretation centering on the notion of *Friedlosigkeit*, an absence of peace. The point at issue is the structural character of this form of exclusion in Germanic law. See Maurizio Lupoi and Adrian Belton, *The*

Origins of the European Legal Order (Cambridge: Cambridge University Press, 2007), p. 370.

13. Du Boys, *Histoire du droit criminel des peuples modernes,* p. 545.

14. Quoted in Le Huërou, *Histoire des institutions mérovingiennes,* 96.

15. Du Boys, *Histoire du droit criminel des peuples modernes,* p. 130.

16. Ibid., p. 124.

17. Esprit Fléchier, *Mémoires de Fléchier sur les Grands-Jours d'Auvergne en 1665* (Paris: Hachette, 1856), p. 258.

18. Ernest Lehr, *Éléments de droit civil anglais* (Paris: Larose et Forcel, 1885), p. 19.

19. Jacob, "Bannissement et rite de la langue tirée au Moyen Âge," p. 1039.

20. Du Boys, *Histoire du droit criminel des peuples modernes,* p. 125.

21. Jacob, "Bannissement et rite de la langue tirée au Moyen Âge," p. 1044.

22. Giorgio Agamben, *Homo sacer, vol. 1, Le Pouvoir souverain et la vie nue* (Paris: Seuil, 1997), p. 117.

23. Eric Hobsbawm, *Bandits,* revised edition (New York: New Press, 2000), p. 14.

CHAPTER 4

Hunting Indians

1. *Lives of Vasco Núñez de Balboa and Francisco Pizarro,* trans. Manuel José Quintana (London: Strand, 1832), p. 18.

2. Gonzalo Fernández de Oviedo y Valdés, *Historia general de las Indias,* book 29, chap. 3, quoted in ibid.

3. Brasseur de Bourbourg, *Histoire des nations civilisées du Mexique et de l'Amérique centrale* (Paris: Arthus Bertrand, 1859), vol. 4, p. 523.

4. Alfred Deberle, *Histoire de l'Amérique du Sud depuis la conquête jusqu'à nos jours* (Paris: Alcan, 1897), p. 57.

5. Auguste de Saint-Hilaire, *Voyage dans les provinces de Saint-Paul et de Sainte-Cathérine* (Paris: Arthus Bertrand, 1851), vol. 1, p. 43.

6. Ibid., p. 25.

7. Elias Regnault, *Histoire des Antilles et des colonies françaises, espagnoles, anglaises* (Paris: Didot, 1849), p. 9.

8. Henry Rowe Schoolcraft, *Historical and Statistical Information Respecting the History, Condition and Prospects of the Indian Tribes of the United States*, vol. 3 (Philadelphia: Lippincott, Grambo, 1854), p. 162.

9. David Bailie Warden, "Chronologie historique de l'Amérique," in *L'Art de vérifier les dates*, part 4, vol. 9 (Paris: n.p., 1842), p. 412.

10. Ibid.

11. Charles Darwin, *The Origin of Species and the Voyage of the Beagle* (New York: Knopf, 2003), p. 141.

12. Juan Ginés de Sepúlveda, "Democrates alter, sive de justis belli causis apud Indos," *Boletín de la real academia de historia* 31, no. 4 (1892): 260–369, 293.

13. Ibid., p. 308.

14. An argument consistent with the Aristotelian thesis that the hierarchy of ontological perfections is the basis for a natural order of domination accompanied by a right to coerce. "Matter must obey form; the body, the soul; the appetites, reason; animals, men; women, their husbands; the son, the father; the imperfect, the perfect; the worse, the better." Ibid., p. 348.

15. Ibid., p. 349.

16. Moreover, this is accompanied by an imperative calling for humanitarian conquest: can one abandon to their fate the innocent victims "whom the barbarians sacrifice every year?" No, because "divine law and natural law are binding for all men, who must reject and punish, if possible, the outrages done to other men." Ibid., p. 349. Here the universalist principle of Christian humanism serves as a pretext for conquest, in a schema in which the humanity presently granted to *certain* Indians, but defined purely formally by their position as victims, provides the foundation both for denying the humanity of other Indians and for affirming the moral humanity of their conquerors. A rhetoric of dissociation that makes it possible to establish a connection between the Indians' humanity as victims and the saving humanity of the Europeans.

17. Francis Bacon, *An Advertisement Touching a Holy War* (1622). See *The Works of Francis Bacon* (Philadelphia: Parry & McMillan, 1859), vol. 2, pp. 435–443.

18. Ibid., p. 441.

19. Ibid.

20. Ibid.

21. Ibid.

22. Ibid.

23. Ibid., p. 442.

24. Bacon, in addition to the example of pirates, also cites the hypothetical case of a nation of Amazons "where the whole government, public and private, yea, the militia itself, was in the hands of women. I demand, is not such a preposterous government, against the first order of nature, for women to rule over men, in itself void, and to be suppressed?" Ibid., p. 442. The same reasoning applies to the case of a nation in which slaves reign over their masters, or in which children have ascendency over their fathers. The power of the male, of the master, of the father: these are, in the Aristotelian tradition, the three axes of domination posted as the ontological structure of social humanity.

25. Ibid., p. 441.

26. Ibid., p. 443.

27. "To confiscate the word humanity, to invoke and monopolise such a term, probably has certain incalculable effects, such as denying the enemy the quality of being human and declaring him to be an outlaw of humanity; and a war can thereby be driven to the most extreme inhumanity." Carl Schmitt, *The Concept of the Political*, trans. J. H. Lomax (Chicago: University of Chicago Press, 2007), p. 54.

28. Ibid.

29. Carl Schmitt, *The Nomos of the Earth in the International Law of the Jus Publicum Europaeum*, trans. G. L. Ulmen (New York: Telos Press, 2003), p. 103.

30. Carl Schmitt, *Donoso Cortes in gesamteuropäischer Interpretation* (Cologne: Greven, 1950), p. 108.

31. These are, on the contrary, the representatives of a fundamentalist Catholicism. French reactionaries were quite right when they cited Bacon in opposition to secular humanism and called for new crusades. De Maistre: "An evident and truly divine maxim! For the supremacy of man has no foundation other than his resemblance to God. (Bacon, in *Dial. de bello sacro*)." Joseph de Maistre, *Les Soirées de Saint-Pétersbourg* (Lyon: Pélagaud, 1850), vol. 1, p. 281. Bonald: "Any society in which . . . religion is absurd, in which practices are barbarian or licentious, is not a legitimate society, because it is not in conformity with the will of the father and creator of all societies. I do not make this statement, as bold as it may seem, entirely without support. Bacon has written a special treatise, *De bello sacro*, to prove that Christian powers

could or had to make war on the Turks, whom he calls a people *ex lex*, that is, outside the law of nations." Louis de Bonald, "Sur la Turquie," in *Oeuvres complètes* (Paris: Migne, 1864), vol. 2, pp. 909–913, 909.

32. Samuel von Pufendorf, *Le droit de la nature et des gens* (Leiden: Wetstein, 1771), vol. 2, p. 556.

33. Ibid., p. 552.

34. The confrontation took place in 1550, during the Valladolid controversy.

35. "Répliques de l'évêque de Chiapas," in Nestor Capdevila, *La Controverse entre Las Casas et Sepúlveda* (Paris: Vrin, 2007), pp. 243–288, 282.

36. Bartolomé de Las Casas, *Apologia* (Madrid: Alianza, 1988), p. 101.

37. To the project of conquest by war, Las Casas opposes the example of St. Jude Thaddeus, who, sent to Mesopotamia to "evangelize people whose savage and ferocious nature was like that of animals," drew solely on the pure resources of the faith. And he concludes with this ironic commentary: "This kind of hunting differs from that professed by Aristotle, who in truth, even if he was a great philosopher, is unworthy of being captured by this hunt which allows access to God only through knowledge of the true faith." Ibid., p. 133.

38. This is a classic theme, also in the law of war: one cannot fight in the name of humanity while denying that of one's adversary. One cannot claim to incarnate humanity while showing oneself to be inhumane. That is because, relative to the means of combat, the question of humanity is not only that of the enemy but also and especially that of the fighter. As Pufendorf wrote, the "law of humanity" limits the right to an infinite hostility because "it requires us to consider not only whether this or that act of hostility can be exercised against our enemies, without the latter having reason to complain, but even if they are worthy of a human conqueror." Pufendorf, *Le droit de la nature et des gens*, p. 557.

39. "Here, as is often the case, everyone is fighting in the name of the same values—freedom and justice. What distinguishes them is the kind of men for whom liberty or justice is demanded, and with whom society is to be made—slaves or masters. Machiavelli was right: values are necessary but not sufficient; and it is even dangerous to stop with values, for as long as we have not chosen those whose mission is to uphold these values in the historical struggle, we have done nothing." Maurice Merleau-Ponty, *Signs*, trans. R. C. McCleary (Evanston, IL: Northwestern University Press, 1964), pp. 220–221.

CHAPTER 5
Hunting Black Skins

1. Charles Athanase Walckenaer, *Histoire générales des voyages* (Paris: Lefèvre, 1826), vol. 1, p. 68.

2. Ibid.

3. Ibid.

4. Ibid.

5. Ibid., p. 70.

6. J. H. Bentley and H. F. Ziegler, *Traditions and Encounters: A Global Perspective on the Past* (Boston: McGraw-Hill, 2003), p. 703.

7. Kabolo Iko Kabwita, *Le Royaume Kongo et la mission catholique* (Wetteren: J. De Meester et Fils, 1929), p. 170.

8. Ibid., p. 103.

9. Dieudonné Rinchon, *La traite et l'esclavage des Congolais par les Européens* (Wetteren: J. De Meester et Fils, 1929), p. 170.

10. Louis-Marie-Joseph Olivier de Grandpré, *Voyage à la côte d'Afrique* (Paris: Dentu, 1801), p. 212.

11. Kabolo Iko Kabwita, *Le Royaume Kongo et la mission catholique*, p. 104.

12. Ibid.

13. Father Moinet, quoted by Georges Leblond, *À l'assaut des pays nègres* (Paris: Oeuvre des Écoles d'Orient, 1884), p. 316.

14. For a summary of this line of argument, see William Snelgrave, *Nouvelle relation de quelques endroits de Guinée et du commerce d'esclaves* (Amsterdam: Au dépens de la Compagnie, 1735), p. 189.

15. Anthony Benezet, *Some Historical Account of Guinea* (London: Owen, 1772), p. 60.

16. Honoré Gabriel Riqueti, comte de Mirabeau, "Discours sur l'abolition de la traite des noirs," in Marcel Dorigny, ed., *Les Bières flottantes des négriers* (Saint-Étienne: Publications de l'Université de Saint-Étienne, 2006), p. 65.

17. Charles Levasseur, *Esclavage de la race noire aux colonies françaises* (Paris: Bajat, 1840), p. 84. "Negroland," or Negritia, was an area in central West Africa, between Guinea and the Sahara.

18. Ibid.

19. André Brue, cited in Benezet, *Some Historical Account of Guinea*, p. 109.

20. Jules Barthélemy-Saint-Hilaire, in his commentary on Aristotle's *Politics* (Paris: Imprimerie Royale, 1837), vol. 1, p. 17.

21. Julien Joseph Virey, "Nègres," in *Nouveau dictionnaire d'histoire naturelle* (Paris: Chez Deterville, 1816–1819), vol. 23, p. 436.

22. Quoted in Levasseur, *Esclavage de la race noire aux colonies françaises*, p. 82.

23. Voltaire, *The Works of Voltaire: Ancient and Modern History* (Paris: E. R. Dumont, 1901), p. 138.

24. Ibid.

25. Ibid., p. 805.

26. G. W. F. Hegel, *Principles of the Philosophy of Right*, trans. S. W. Dyde (Kitchener, Ontario: Batoche, 2001), p. 66.

27. However, this does not mean that Hegel was unaware of the violence of the slave-trade system: "As in a slave-ship, the crew is constantly armed and the greatest care is taken to prevent an insurrection, so the Spartans exercised constant vigilance over the Helots, and were always in a condition of war, as against enemies." G. W. F. Hegel, *Lectures on the Philosophy of History*, trans. Hugh Barr Nisbet (Cambridge: Cambridge University Press, 1981), p. 273.

28. G. W. F. Hegel, *Vorlesungen über die Philosophie des Rechtes: Berlin, 1819–1820* (Hamburg: Meiner, 2000), p. 22.

29. David Brion Davis praises Hegel's genius and sums up his fundamental teaching as follows: "We can expect nothing from the mercy of God or from the mercy of those who exercise worldly lordship in His or other names; that man's true emancipation, whether physical or spiritual, must always depend on those who have endured and overcome some form of slavery." David Brion Davis, *The Problem of Slavery in the Age of Revolution* (New York: Oxford University Press, 1999), p. 564.

30. G. W. F. Hegel, *Die Philosophie der Geschichte: Vorlesungsmitschrift Heimann (Winter 1830/1831)* (Munich: Fink, 2005), p. 70.

31. On this subject, see this other passage: "The negroes are enslaved by the Europeans and sold to America. Nevertheless, their lot in their own country, where slavery is equally absolute, is almost worse than this; for the basic principle of all slavery is that man is not yet conscious of his freedom." Hegel, *Lectures on the Philosophy of History*, p. 183.

32. This text of Hegel's leads us to have strong reservations regarding the interpretation proposed by Susan Buck-Morss in *Hegel, History, and Universal History* (Pittsburgh: University of Pittsburgh Press, 2009).

33. Elsewhere, after having asserted that "one of the main ambitions of the kings is to sell their captured enemies or even their own subjects, and, to this extent at least, slavery has awakened more humanity among the negroes," Hegel concludes: "Thus it is more fitting and correct that slavery should be eliminated gradually than that it should be done away with all at once." Hegel, *Lectures on the Philosophy of History*, pp. 183–184.

34. G. W. F. Hegel, *Philosophy of Mind*, trans. W. Wallace (Oxford: Clarendon, 1971), p. 175.

35. Hegel, *Lectures on the Philosophy of History*, p. 185.

36. "The Negro is an example of animal man in all his savagery and lawlessness" Hegel, *Lectures on the Philosophy of History*, p. 177.

37. "They do not have the consciousness that man is inherently free. Family love is weak or even nonexistent. The son sells his parents, his sisters, his wife, and his children. Contrary to any ethical consideration, slavery is widespread. Man has no value in himself. We cannot speak of contempt for death, but there exists among them a nonconsideration of life insofar as they have no ethical goal. Death means nothing to them. They die heedlessly." Hegel, *Die Philosophie der Geschichte: Vorlesungsmitschrift Heimann (Winter 1830/1831)*, p. 69.

38. G. W. F. Hegel, *Lectures on the Philosophy of Religion,* trans. R. F. Brown et al. (Berkeley: University of California Press, 1984–1987), vol. 2, p. 297

39. Ottobah Cugoano, *Thoughts and Sentiments on the Evil and Wicked Traffic of the Slavery*, in Francis D. Adams, *Three Black Writers in Eighteenth Century England* (Belmont, CA: Wadsworth, 1971), p. 95.

CHAPTER 6
The Dialectic of the Hunter and the Hunted

1. Gomes Eanes de Zurara, *Chronique de Guinée* (Dakar: IFAN, 1960), p. 99.

2. "The animal, for me, is a being that is fundamentally on its guard." Gilles Deleuze, in "A comme Animal," from the series *L'Abécédaire de Gilles Deleuze* (video recording, Paris: Éditions Montparnasse, 1997).

3. "The Interesting Narrative of the Life of Olaudah Equiano," in William L. Andrews and Henry Louis Gates, eds., *Slave Narratives* (New York: Library of America, 2000), p. 68. Equiano cites here

two verses from the poem "Cooper's Hill," by the English writer John Denham.

4. Ottobah Cugoano, *Thoughts and Sentiments on the Evil and Wicked Traffic of the Slavery*, in Francis D. Adams, *Three Black Writers in Eighteenth Century England* (Belmont, CA: Wadsworth, 1971), p. 32. When collective revolt was not possible, "individual resistance usually took the form of attempted suicide . . . . One prominent way was to refuse to eat." The crew then made use of "the *speculum orum*, a screwlike device that forced the mouth open and allowed the crew to force-feed recalcitrant Africans." Junius P. Rodriguez, ed., *Encyclopedia of Slave Resistance and Rebellion* (Westport, CT: Greenwood, 2007), p. 323.

5. Suicides occurred every time the rebellious slaves were cornered in a situation from which there was no escape. Elsa Dorlin cites the fugitives at Saint Thomas, who were "so frightened by the French's continual manhunts that they all swore an oath to kill themselves," and whose bodies were found in the woods, "all in the same position: lined up alongside one another, each one holding a rifle to the temple of his neighbor." Elsa Dorlin, "Les Espaces-temps des résistances esclaves: Des suicidés de Saint-Jean aux marrons de Nanny Town (XVIIe–XVIIIe siècles)," *Tumultes*, no. 27 (2006): 37–54.

6. See, for example, Frederick Douglass, *Autobiographies* (New York: Library of America, 1994), p. 324.

7. Cf. *White Zombie* (1932), directed by Victor Halperin, with Bela Lugosi in the role of the master, and the updating of this motif in George A. Romero's *Night of the Living Dead* (1968), with the final manhunt scene in which the black character, having escaped zombification, is shot down by white hunters: either life as one of the living dead or death in the attempt to escape, those are the only alternatives left to the black consciousness.

8. *Revenge of the Zombies* (1943), directed by Steve Sekeley. The screenplay made a twofold shift: the role of the black slave was transferred to a white woman, and that of the American slave-master to a Nazi scientist played by John Carradine.

9. Orlando Patterson, *Slavery or Social Death: A Comparative Study* (Cambridge, MA: Harvard University Press, 1982), p. 98.

10. Ibid.

11. Douglass, *Autobiographies*, p. 283.

12. Paul Gilroy, *The Black Atlantic: Modernity and Double Consciousness* (Cambridge, MA: Harvard University Press, 1993), p. 60.

13. Gilroy mentions "this turn toward death as a release from terror and bondage. . . . Douglass's preference for death fits readily with archival material on the practice of slave suicide." Ibid., p. 95. But, as Laura Chrisman points out, by doing so Gilroy "seems over-quick to convert a willingness to risk death into a positive orientation, a desire for death." Laura Chrisman, *Postcolonial Contraventions* (Manchester: Manchester University Press, 2003), p. 83. But there is a major difference between choosing to risk death in order to live free and choosing to die in order to remain free in death, which prohibits us from conflating a fight to the death with an intent to commit suicide, even if only because, in accord with a classical philosophical distinction, we are not in the former case the agent of our own deaths.

14. The expression is quoted by Schoelcher, who refers to this "crime of stealing their cadavers, as the negroes say." Victor Schoelcher, *Histoire de l'esclavage pendant les deux dernières années* (Paris: Pagnerre, 1847), p. 447.

15. Ibid., p. 449. Schoelcher chronicled escapes, day by day, as a kind of refutation: "20 August 1846: Escape of 30 slaves in Guadeloupe. A great audacity." Ibid., p. 447.

16. "Marron ou Cimarron?" in Bory de Saint-Vincent et al., eds., *Dictionnaire classique d'histoire naturelle* (Paris: Rey et Gravier, 1826), vol. 10, p. 193.

17. Amédée Villard, *Histoire de l'esclavage ancien et moderne par A. Tourmagne* (Paris: Guillaumin, 1880), p. 328. See also Francisco Estévez, *La Rancheador: Journal d'un chasseur d'esclaves. Cuba, 1837–1842* (Paris: Taillandier, 2008).

18. The *quilombos* were maroon slave camps hidden in the back country. See Mário José Maestri Filho, Mário Maestri, and Florence Carboni, *L'Esclavage au Brésil* (Paris: Karthala, 1991), p. 152.

19. "Marron ou Cimarron?" p. 193.

20. An announcement that appeared in the *New York Daily Tribune* for 21 February 1857, quoted in Auguste Carlier, *De l'Esclavage dans ses rapports avec l'union américaine* (Paris: Lévy, 1862), p. 290.

21. In sixteenth-century Peru, more than half the *caudrilleros*, "a kind of rural police one of whose functions was to hunt down and arrest fugitive slaves, . . . were free blacks and mulattos who received wages." Carmen Bernand and Alessandro Stella, *D'Esclaves à soldats: Miliciens et soldats d'origine servile, XIIIe–XXIe siècles* (Paris: Harmattan, 2006), p. 88

22. "Discours de Guadet sur les colonies," 23 March 1792, in *Archives parlementaires de 1787 à 1860* (N.p.: n.p., 1893), vol. 40, p. 409.

23. Patterson, *Slavery or Social Death*, p. 101.

24. Here is how the training proceeded: "The puppy having been deprived of food, meat was placed where the dog could reach it in the belly of a dummy painted black: as soon as the dummy fell into the dog's cage, he leapt on it and tore it to pieces. . . . Then these figures were given a more precise resemblance to negroes; they were made to move at a distance, giving them all the movements of a man; they were brought near the cage where the starving animal was confined. The latter threw itself at the bars, tried to seize the prey, and barked furiously. Finally, when its fury and appetite had been equally excited, it was set free; it ran to its victim, which the instructors made struggle in simulated efforts to escape the dog's pitiless jaws." Elias Regnault, *Histoire des Antilles et des colonies françaises, espagnoles, anglaises* (Paris: Didot, 1849), p. 102.

25. An announcement that appeared on 6 November 1845, quoted in Carlier, *De l'Esclavage dans ses rapports avec l'union américaine*, p. 292. Indefatigable, strong, and fast, endowed with an exceptional sense of smell, these dogs left the fugitives little chance to escape. The slave William W. Brown tells of his capture: "One day, while in the woods, I heard the barking and howling of dogs, and in a short time they came so near that I knew them to be the bloodhounds of Major Benjamin O'Fallon. He kept five or six, to hunt runaway slaves with.—As soon as I was convinced that it was them, I knew there was no chance of escape." Andrews and Gates, *Slave Narratives*, p. 280.

26. Joseph Elzéar Morénas, *Précis historique de la traite des noirs* (Paris: Firmin Didot, 1828), p. 87.

27. Andrews and Gates, *Slave Narratives*, p. 696.

28. "It is pleasure in war, but no longer the immediate delight in manhunting." Norbert Elias, "On Transformations of Aggressiveness," *Theory and Society* 5, no. 2 (1978): 229–242, 234.

29. Norbert Elias and Eric Dunning, *Quest for Excitement: Sport and Leisure in the Civilizing Process* (Oxford: Blackwell, 1986), p. 166.

30. Régis de Trobriand, *Quatre ans de campagnes à l'Armée du Potomac* (Paris: Librairie internationale, 1867), p. 180.

31. Ibid.

32. Aimé Césaire, *Discourse on Colonialism* (New York: Monthly Review Press, 1972), p. 35.

33. Jean-Paul Sartre, *Theory of Practical Ensembles*, vol. 1 of *Critique of Dialectical Reason*, trans. A. Sheridan-Smith (London: NLB, 1976), pp. 515–516.

34. Thomas Hobbes, *Treatise on Human Nature* (London: J. Johnson, 1812), p. 25.

35. Andrews and Gates, *Slave Narratives*, p. 533.

36. Jean Baptiste Le Verrier de La Conterie, *L'École de la chasse aux chiens courants ou Vénerie normande* (Paris: Bouchard-Huzard, 1845), p. 463.

37. Prosper Ève, *Les Esclaves de Bourbon: La mer et la montagne* (Paris: Karthala, 2003), p. 224.

38. Alexander von Humboldt, *Examen critique de l'histoire et de la géographie du nouveau continent* (Paris: Gide, 1837), vol. 3, p. 374

39. Bryan Edwards, *Histoire abrégée des nègres-marrons de la Jamaïque*, quoted in *Bibliothèque britannique* (Geneva: Imprimerie de la bibliothèque britannique, 1804), vol. 26, p. 39.

40. Ibid., p. 49.

41. In the nineteenth century, in a different context, French readers were thus able to delight in the exploits of the canine brigade employed against the natives in Algeria: "I knew the famous Blanchette, the Attila of Kabylia, the most noble expression of canine bravery, a great white greyhound who walked on only three legs, having lost the fourth in a fight with an enemy chief." Alphonse Toussenel, *L'Esprit des bêtes: Vénerie française et zoologie passionnelle* (Paris: Librairie sociétaire, 1847), p. 169.

42. Charles Expilly, *La Traite, l'émigration et la colonisation au Brésil* (Paris: Lacroix, 1865), p. 212.

43. *Mémoire autographe du général Ramel sur l'expédition de Saint-Domingue*, quoted in Victor Schoelcher, *Vie de Toussaint Louverture* (Paris: Karthala, 1982), p. 373.

44. Regnault, *Histoire des Antilles et des colonies françaises, espagnoles, anglaises*, p. 69.

45. The film was made in 1932 at R.K.O., by Irving Pichel and Ernest B. Schoedsack, based on the short story of the same name by Richard Connell. The title plays on the double meaning of *game*.

46. First version of a passage attributed to Diderot in Guillaume Raynal, *A Philosophical and Political History of the Settlements and Trade of the Europeans in the East and West Indies* (London: Cadell, 1777), vol. 3, p. 466.

47. Directed by David A. Prior (1988).

48. Mikhail Bakunin, "Statuts secrets de l'Alliance: Programme et objet de l'organisation révolutionnaire des Frères internationaux" (autumn 1868), in Daniel Guérin, *Ni Dieu ni maître: Anthologie historique du mouvement anarchiste* (Lausanne: La Cité, 1969), p. 229.

CHAPTER 7
Hunting the Poor

1. Michel Foucault, *Madness and Civilization* (London: Routledge, 2001), p. 45.

2. Charles Antoine Parmentier, *Archives de Nevers ou Inventaire historique des titres de la ville* (Paris: Techner, 1842), vol. 1, p. 144.

3. Christian Paultre, *De la répression de la mendicité et du vagabondage en France sous l'ancien régime* (Paris: L. Larose & L. Tenin, 1906), p. 532.

4. Ibid., p. 267.

5. Ibid., p. 532.

6. Before being expelled, beggars might be employed in public works that were as unattractive as they were suited to the beggars' condition, given their supposed natural affinity with dirt and filth: cleaning the sewers, picking up garbage, constructing fortifications. In Paris, the regulations for the Great Poor Office issued in 1586 provided that the poor would be "employed in cleaning up the dirt and filth of the city . . . things that are very necessary to drive all the incorrigible idlers and poor out of Paris and to give them a reason to leave the aforesaid city." Ibid., p. 266.

7. Antoine Furetière, *Les Mots obsolètes* (Paris: Zulma, 1998), p. 71.

8. François Naville, *De la charité légale, de ses effets, de ses causes* (Paris: Dufart, 1836), vol. 2, p. 25.

9. Michel Foucault, *History of Madness*, trans. J. Murphy and J. Khalfa (New York: Routledge, 2006), pp. 63–64.

10. *Foreigner* meaning here from outside the province or the city, without reference to nationality.

11. *Mémoires de l'Académie des sciences, arts et belles-lettres de Dijon* (Dijon: Frantin, 1832), p. 56.

12. Jules Loiseleur, *Les Crimes et les Peines dans l'Antiquité et dans les temps modernes* (Paris: Hachette, 1863), p. 253.

13. André Zysberg, Les galères de France sous le règne de Louis XIV. Essai de comptabilité globale," in Martine Acerra, José Merino, and Jean Meyer, eds., Les Marines de guerre européennes: XVIIe–XVIIIe siècles (Paris: Presses de l'Université de Paris–Sorbonne, 1998), pp. 415–444, 430.

14. Loiseleur, Les Crimes et les Peines dans l'Antiquité et dans les temps modernes, p. 252.

15. Naville, De la charité légale, de ses effets, de ses causes, p. 9.

16. Emmanuel Le Roy Ladurie, Les Paysans de Languedoc (Paris: Éditions de l'École des hautes études en sciences sociales, 1966), p. 94.

17. Paultre, De la répression de la mendicité et du vagabondage en France sous l'ancien régime, p. 195.

18. Ibid., p. 266.

19. Alban Villeneuve-Bargemon, Économie politique chrétienne, ou Recherche sur la nature et les causes du paupérisme (Brussels: Meline, Cans, 1837), p. 371.

20. Alexandre Monnier, Histoire de l'assistance publique dans les temps anciens et modernes (Paris: Guillaumin, 1866), p. 522.

21. Alexandre Dumas, Parisiens et provinciaux (Paris: Lévy, 1868), vol. 1, p. 286.

22. J. H. Rosny, L'Impérieuse bonté: Roman contemporain (Paris: Plon-Nourrit, 1894), p. 212.

23. "Charité," in Jean Baptiste Glaire and Joseph-Alexis Walsh, eds., Encyclopédie catholique, vol. 6 (Paris: Parent-Desbarres, 1843), p. 503.

24. Foucault, History of Madness, p. 62.

25. Quoted in Alphonse Jobez, La France sous Louis XV (Paris: Didier, 1873), p. 262.

26. Louis Andrieux, Souvenirs d'un préfet de police (Paris: J. Rouff, 1885), vol. 1, p. 65.

27. Yves Guyot, La Police (Paris: Charpentier, 1884), p. 275.

28. Michel Foucault, Foucault Live (New York: Semiotexte, 1996), p. 84.

CHAPTER 8
Police Hunts

1. Paul Viller, "Le chien, gardien de la société," Je sais tout, no. 33 (15 October 1907): 361–368, 368.

2. "La Police et les voleurs de Londres," Revue britannique 2 (1856): 257–276, 265.

3. Alphonse Bertillon, *Signaletic Instructions* (New York: Werner, 1896), pp. 6–7.

4. Ibid. p. 6.

5. "Sans casque, ni bouclier: Témoignage d'un ex-officier de police," http://regardeavue.com/index.php/2006/05/21/10-sanscasque-ni -bouclier-temoignagedun-ex-officier-de-police.

6. Honoré de Balzac, *Balzac in Twenty-five Volumes* (New York: Collier, 1900), p. 113.

7. Maxime du Camp, *Paris, ses organes, ses fonctions et sa vie dans la seconde moitié du XIXe siècle* (Paris: Hachette, 1879), p. 100.

8. Eugène-François Vidocq, *Mémoires de Vidocq, chef de la police de sûreté jusqu'en 1827* (Paris: Huillery, 1868), p. 5.

9. Ibid., p. 267.

10. *Discussion du projet de loi sur les prisons à la Chambre des députés* (Paris: Au bureau de la revue pénitenciaire, 1844), p. 632.

11. *La Presse*, 26 August 1836, quoted in Louis Moreau-Christophe, *Défense du projet de loi sur les prisons* (Paris: Au bureau de la revue pénitenciaire, 1844), p. 40.

12. Ibid.

13. Almire Lepelletier de la Sarthe, *Système pénitentiaire complet* (Paris: Guillaumin, 1857), p. 472.

14. Ibid., p. 473.

15. Emile Zola, *Les Trois Villes* (Paris: Gallimard, 2002), p. 245.

16. See John McQuilton, *The Kelly Outbreak, 1878–1880: The Geographical Dimension of Social Banditry* (Carlton: Melbourne University Press, 1979). I thank Aude Fauvel for drawing my attention to this wonderful Australian story.

17. For example, someone who refuses to honor Caesar or who plans an attack on his life is counted a public enemy. Originally, "enemies described as 'public' could only be internal enemies, opponents who represented or had represented a threat to the imperial power." Anne Daguet-Gagey, "C. Fuluius Plautianus, hostis publicus, Rome 205–208 après J.C.," in Marie-Henriette Quet, *La "crise" de l'Empire romain de Marc Aurèle à Constantin* (Paris: PUPS, 2006), pp. 65–94, 77.

18. Ibid., p. 81.

19. Jean-Jacques Rousseau, *Du contrat social* (Paris: Garnier, 1975), book 2, chap. 5, p. 257.

20. Elliott J. Gorn, *Dillinger's Wild Ride: The Year That Made America's Public Enemy Number One* (New York: Oxford University Press, 2009), p. 153.

21. Claire Bond Potter, *War on Crime: Bandits, G-men, and the Politics of Mass Culture* (New Brunswick, NJ: Rutgers University Press, 1998), p. 139.

22. Is it an accident that in France, in the nineteenth century, the generals who put down workers' insurrections had almost all served their military apprenticeships in the armies of Africa? Galliffet, the butcher of the Commune, and Cavaignac, who had crushed the workers' revolt that Bugeaud had failed to stop, had both fought in Algeria. Bugeaud, whose name remains associated with the massacre in the Rue Transnonain in Paris and who was still active in Paris in 1848, was one of the generals from Africa who promoted the policy of smoking out the adversary. In Pélissier, on 11 June 1845, he had written: "If these rascals withdraw into their caves, imitate Cavaignac at the Sbeahs: smoke them out like foxes." Charles Tailliart, *L'Algérie dans la littérature française* (Paris: E. Champion, 1925), p. 232. Émile Pouget established this connection between colonial wars and the ferocity of internal repression on the basis of a political solidarity, later denouncing the French exactions in Tonkin: "Who are you, where do you come from, you dirty bastards, you weren't born yesterday, were you? I saw you eighteen years ago, and your mug hasn't changed: you're still from Versailles! The ferociousness of tiger cats that you've used to torment the Communards you're using now to torment the Tonkinois." Émile Pouget, "Barbarie française," *Le Père peinard*, no. 45 (12 January 1890).

23. Louis Ménard, *Prologue d'une révolution: Février–juin 1848* (Paris: La Fabrique, 2007), p. 154.

In this connection, Gallois alludes to *cryptia*: "Excitement and fury seizes these men full of hate, and one sees among them amateurs carrying game-bags and double-barreled guns, indulging in the pleasure of hunting helots." Léonard Gallois, *Histoire de la révolution de 1848* (Paris: Naud, 1851), vol. 2, p. 19.

24. Walter Benjamin, *Das Passagen-Werk* (Frankfurt am Main: Suhrkamp, 1982), p. 951.

CHAPTER 9
The Hunting Pack and Lynching

1. Gilles Deleuze, class at the University of Paris–Vincennes, 12 February 1973.

2. Elias Canetti, *Crowds and Power*, trans. Carol Stewart (New York: Continuum, 1982), p. 96.

3. Ibid., p. 97.

4. Howard Kester, "The Lynching of Claude Neal," quoted in McKay Jenkins, *The South in Black and White: Race, Sex, and Literature in the 1940s* (Chapel Hill: University of North Carolina Press, 1999), p. 49.

5. Ibid., p. 50.

6. Gustave Le Bon, *Psychologie des foules* (Paris: PUF, 1947), p. 39.

7. Frederick Douglass, "The Lesson of the Hour" (1894), in David B. Chesebrough, *Frederick Douglass: Oratory from Slavery* (Westport, CT: Greenwood Press, 1998), pp. 134–143, 141.

8. Ibid., p. 134.

9. At the very time that feminist demands were increasing in power, this ideology that made masculine violence the prerogative of racified men thus provided a powerful instrument for setting against each other, in the battle for civil rights, the struggles of white women and those of black people.

10. Robyn Wiegman, "The Anatomy of Lynching," *Journal of the History of Sexuality* 3, no. 3 (1993): 445–467, 461.

11. See Richard Maxwell Brown, *Strain of Violence: Historical Studies of American Violence and Vigilantism* (New York: Oxford University Press, 1975), p. 151.

12. Cited in Hadley Cantril, *The Psychology of Social Movements* (New Brunswick, NJ: Transaction, 2002), p. 115.

13. Oliver C. Cox, *Caste, Class, and Race: A Study in Social Dynamics* (New York: Monthly Review Press, 1959), p. 558.

CHAPTER 10
Hunting Foreigners

1. *Le Petit Méridional*, 18 August 1893.

2. Testimony published in *Il Secolo*, 22–23 August 1893, quoted in Enzo Barnabà, *Le Sang des marais, Aigues-Mortes 17 août 1893, une tragédie de l'immigration italienne* (Marseilles: Via Valeriano, 1993).

3. Napoleone Colajanni, *Una questione ardente, la concorrenza del lavoro* (Rome: Biblioteca delle rivista popolare, 1893), quoted in Barnabà, *Le Sang des marais*.

4. This in the context of what the economist Edna Bonacich calls "a split labor market," in which two fractions of the labor force pre-

sent a differential in terms of the cost of labor for the same task, and in which, if they are distinguished by national origin, putting them in competition with each other may result in ethnic antagonism. One of the possible strategies for the group of workers whose labor cost is higher is *exclusion*, which "tries to prevent the physical presence of cheaper labor in the employment area." Edna Bonacich, "A Theory of Ethnic Antagonism: The Split Labor Market," *American Sociological Review* 37, no. 5 (1972): 547–559, 555. The other strategy is that of the maintenance of caste privileges. While the first strategy consists in expelling undesirables (a violent movement of exclusion), the second is characterized by the previously described phenomena of hunting and lynching (a violent reassertion of ethnosocial caste privilege within a system of domination).

5. Quoted in Michel-Louis Rouquette, *La Chasse à l'immigré: Violence, mémoire et représentations* (Sprimont: Mardaga, 1997), p. 32.

6. Ibid., p. 22.

7. Maurice Barrès, *Contre les étrangers. Étude pour la protection des ouvriers français* (Paris: Grande imprimerie parisienne, 1893).

8. Maurice Barrès, *Scènes et doctrines du nationalisme* (Paris: Plon-Nourrit, 1925), vol. 3, p. 161.

9. Ibid., p. 164.

10. Frédéric Bastiat, *Mélanges d'économie politique* (Brussels: Méline, Cans, 1851), vol. 1, p. 152. On the history of these debates, see the excellent essay by Pierre-Jacques Derainne, "Migrations de travail, conflits et sociabilités: L'Exemple des ouvriers allemands en France sous la monarchie de Juillet et la seconde République," in *Deutsche Handwerker, Arbeiter und Dienstmädchen in Paris. Eine vergessene migration im 19.Jahrhundert* (Munich: Oldenbourg, 2003), pp. 121–142.

11. So equality became another name for free and undistorted competition, a paradox that Marx commented on as follows: "To call cosmopolitan exploitation universal brotherhood is an idea that could only be engendered in the brain of the bourgeoisie." Karl Marx, "Address on Free Trade," in Marx, *The Poverty of Philosophy* (London: Martin Lawrence, 1936), p. 207.

12. As Pierre-Jacques Derainne demonstrates, it was, in fact, "under the July Monarchy and the Second Republic that the whole contemporary argument about national preference in matters of employment began to be developed in France and to spread among the workers and the bourgeoisie." Derainne, "Migrations de travail, conflits et sociabilités," p. 141.

13. "Sur la liberté des échanges—A Monsieur Frédéric Bastiat," *L'Atelier: Organe spécial de la classe laborieuse*, October 1846, pp. 387–389, 388.

14. Ibid.

15. Foreign workers were expelled from the workshops, and some political groups tried to launch a campaign of xenophobic agitation. One Saturday in April 1848, Parisian workers, whom posters had called to a public meeting, "saw an individual appear who, after having unfurled a flag, read them a violent proclamation urging them to drive all foreign workers out of France. Rightly scandalized by such a suggestion, the workers who formed the crowd, two to three hundred of them, seized the man and took him to the police station." *L'Ami de la religion*, 11 April 1848, p. 107.

16. "Correspondance," *L'Atelier: Organe spécial des ouvriers*, 12 April 1848, p. 119.

17. Ibid.

18. Ibid.

19. Bernard Lazare, *Juifs et antisémites* (Paris: Allia, 1992), p. 77.

CHAPTER 11
Hunting Jews

1. The Pastoureaux, whose name means literally "little shepherds," were peasants who developed, in the thirteenth and fourteenth centuries, a popular movement whose declared goal was to liberate the Holy Land.

2. Alexandre Du Mège, *Histoire générale de Languedoc* (Toulouse: Paya, 1844), vol. 7, p. 70.

3. Baruch, having been baptized by force, was later put on trial by the Inquisition. This testimony is taken from his interrogation. See *Le Registre d'inquisition de Jacques Fournier, évêque de Pamiers (1318–1325)*, ed. and trans. Jean Duvernoy (Paris: Mouton, 1978), vol. 1, p. 224.

4. Hannah Arendt, *The Origins of Totalitarianism* (New York: Harcourt, Brace & World, 1966), p. 7.

5. Du Mège, *Histoire générale de Languedoc*, p. 70.

6. David Nirenberg, *Communities of Violence: Persecution of Minorities in the Middle Ages* (Princeton, NJ: Princeton University Press, 1998), p. 48.

7. Ibid., p. 50.

8. Jules Michelet, *Histoire de France* (Paris: Chamerot, 1861), vol. 3, p. 96.

9. Bernard Lazare, *Anti-Semitism: Its History and Causes* (New York: International Publishing Co., 1903), p. 200.

10. Helmut Berding, *Histoire de l'antisémitisme en Allemagne* (Paris: Éditions MSH, 1991), p. 62.

11. Ibid., p. 60.

12. Ibid., p. 61.

13. Abram Leon, *The Jewish Question: A Marxist Interpretation* (N.p.: Pioneras, 1950), p. 201.

14. Édouard Drumont, *La France juive* (Paris: C. Marpon & F. Flammarion, 1887), p. 60.

15. Ibid., pp. 83–85.

16. Ibid., p. 85.

17. Louis-Ferdinand Céline, *Bagatelles pour un massacre: Texte intégral* (Paris: Denoël, 1937), p. 156.

18. Ibid. To this kind of national mythology, based on the absurdity of the historical continuity of an original race, Bernard Lazare replied: "Let's grant the Gauls. So we will cry: Gaul for the Gauls! And the Latins, and the Franks, and the Visigoths, and the Suevi, and the Alamanni? They are vile conquerors, and the old Gauls should rise up and drive them off their territory. The problem is that the old Gauls have been so mixed with the other races—even with the Jews—that no one could find them again." Bernard Lazare, *Juifs et antisémites* (Paris: Allia, 1992), p. 25.

19. Bernard Goldstein, *Five Years in the Warsaw Ghetto*, trans. and ed. Leonard Shatzkin (Edinburgh, WV: AK Press, 2005), p. 44.

20. Ibid., p. 45.

21. J. Ernest-Charles, "La presse et les préoccupations nationales," *Revue bleue*, 4th series, 14 (1863): 378–380, 379.

22. Jacques Bouveresse, "Kraus, Spengler et le déclin de l'Occident," in *Essais II. L'époque, la mode, la morale, la satire* (Marseilles: Agone, 2001), pp. 32–33.

23. Michel Foucault, *"Il faut défendre la société"* (Paris: Gallimard/Seuil, 1997), p. 227.

24. Adolf Hitler, *Monologe im Führer-Hauptquartier, 1941–1944* (Hamburg: A. Knaus, 1980), p. 148.

CHAPTER 12
Hunting Illegals

1. Baba Traoré, who drowned in the Marne River at Joinville-le-Pont, died on 4 April 2008.

2. Derrida commented on this text, emphasizing the "paradoxes of this man-hunt" of which Cain is the target: "Having fallen into the trap and killed Abel, Cain covers himself with shame and flees, wandering, hunted, tracked in turn like a beast. God then promises this human beast protection and vengeance." Jacques Derrida, "The Animal That Therefore I Am (More to Follow)," trans. David Wills, *Critical Inquiry* 28, no. 2 (2002): 369–418, 378.

3. Theodoret, *Quaestiones in Genesim*, XLII, quoted in Monique Alexandre, *Le Commencement du Livre. Genèse I–V, la version grecque de la Septante et sa réception* (Paris: Beauchesne,1988), p. 363.

4. Hannah Arendt, *The Origins of Totalitarianism* (New York: Meridian, 1958), p. 302.

5. Ibid.

6. There is something disconcerting about this from the point of view of juridical logic. "Jurists are so used to thinking of law in terms of punishment, which indeed always deprives us of certain rights, that they may find it even more difficult than the layman to recognize that the deprivation of legality, i.e., of all rights, no longer has a connection with specific crimes." Ibid., p. 295.

7. "The nation-state, incapable of providing a law for those who had lost the protection of a national government, transferred the whole matter to the police. This was the first time the police in Western Europe had received authority to act on its own, to rule directly over people." Ibid., p. 287.

8. Ibid., p. 297.

9. Ibid., p. 302.

10. Hannah Arendt, *The Jew as Pariah: Jewish Identity and Politics in the Modern Age* (New York: Grove, 1978), p. 65.

11. The concept of illegalization was created by Nicholas De Genova. See Nicholas P. De Genova, "Migrant 'Illegality' and Deportability in Everyday Life," *Annual Review of Anthropology* 31 (2002): 419–447.

12. Karine Michelet, *Les droits sociaux des étrangers* (Paris: L'Harmattan, 2002).

13. The medieval principle of territorial sovereignty was expressed in the formula *quidquid est in territorio est de territorio*. This maxim

meant that the sovereign reigned over the whole territory and over everything in it. The principle was then interpreted freely, making it the principle of protecting refugees: "*Qui est in territorio est de territorio.* The foreigner being subject to the laws of the country where he resides, he must also enjoy the protection and the advantages of these same laws." Ivan Golovin, *Esprit de l'économie politique* (Paris: Didot, 1843), p. 382. See also Hannah Arendt, *The Origins of Totalitarianism*, p. 280.

14. Article L622-1 of the Code de l'entrée et du séjour des étrangers et du droit d'asile (Law Governing the Entrance and Residence of Foreigners and the Right of Asylum).

15. *La lettre d'Act Up–Paris*, no. 116, February 2009.

16. Amnesty International, *Vivre dans l'ombre. Les droits des migrants*, December 2006.

17. www.usc.edu/libraries/archives/ethnicstudies/historicdocs/prop187.txt.

18. Nicholas De Genova, *Working the Boundaries: Race, Space, and "Illegality" in Mexican Chicago* (Durham, NC: Duke University Press, 2005), p. 234.

19. De Genova, "Migrant 'Illegality' and Deportability in Everyday Life," p. 429.

20. Judith Butler and Gayatri Chakravorty Spivak, *Who Sings the Nation State* (New York: Seagull, 2007), p. 41.

21. Ibid., p. 42.

22. Karl Marx, *The Holy Family, or, Critique of Critical Critique* (Moscow: Foreign Languages Publishing House, 1956), p. 158.

23. "M. Guillemot: 'Cette insécurité est nécessaire,'" *Kashkazi*, no. 44, 15 June 2006, p. 9.

24. "Personne n'est illégal" ("No one is illegal") appeal.

25. Emmanuel Terray, "Quand on veut interpeller des indésirables, il faut aller les chercher là où ils sont," www.ldhtoulon.net/spip.php?article2279.

26. Carine Fouteau, "Un escorteur de la PAF raconte la violence ordinaire des expulsions forcées," *Mediapart*, 12 October 2009, http.mediapart.fr/journal/france/071009/un-escorteur-dela-paf-raconte-la-violenceordinaire-des-expulsions-forcees.

27. Marcel Mauss, *Manual of Ethnography* (New York: Berghahn, 2007), p. 45.

28. Fouteau, "Un escorteur de la PAF raconte la violence ordinaire des expulsions forcées."

29. Jean-Marc Manach, "Les 'Doigts brûlés' de Calais," *La Valise diplomatique*, 25 September 2009, http.mondediplomatique.fr/carnet/2009-09-25-Calais.

30. Marie Vermillard, "La Mort d'un homme," *Le Monde*, 7 April 2008.

31. Lina Sankari, "Des sans-papiers raflés aux Restos du Coeur," *L'Humanité*, 23 October 2009.

32. "À Belleville, travaux pratiques policiers devant les écoliers," *Libération*, 23 March 2007.

33. La Cimade, "Centres et locaux de rétention administrative—Rapport 2005," *Les hors-séries de Causes Communes*, December 2006.

34. Emmanuel Blanchard, "Ce que rafler veut dire," *Plein droit* 81 (July 2009): 4.

35. As Blanchard reminds us, in France police collaboration marked a radical break with earlier practices: "Administrative internment existed before these years, but in the case of Jews it served to supply the policy of extermination. . . . [T]he 'Spring wind' [*vent printanier*] operation resulted, in the Paris region alone, in the arrest of 13,000 Jews who were first interned in the fifteenth arrondissement, in the Vélodrome d'Hiver, and then in the camp at Drancy, before being transferred to the death camps. The police technique used until the summer of 1942 was not, strictly speaking, part of what was normally done in a police raid. These were in fact arrests made at subjects' homes, thanks to the previous establishment of a file. It was only starting in the 1960s that this police operation, unlike any other in the history of contemporary France, became universally known as the 'rafle du Vél d'Hiv.'" Blanchard, "Ce que rafler veut dire," pp. 5–6.

36. Laurent Decotte, "Fin de la 'jungle' de Calais: Évacuation et communication," *La Voix du Nord*, 23 September 2009.

37. Karl Laske, "Un enfant sans papiers fuit la police et chute du 4e étage," *Libération*, 10 July 2007.

38. French prime minister's website, communiqué of 9 July 2007.

39. Préfecture des Hauts-de-Seine, Direction de la population et de la citoyenneté, *Note aux agents des sections Accueil (guichets pré-accueil) et Contrôle (cellule et régularisation)*, 28 February 2008.

40. Éric Besson was at the time the minister of immigration, integration, and national identity in President Sarkozy's administration.

41. Éric Besson, interviewed by Thomas Legrand, France Inter, 16 October 2009.

CONCLUSION

1. René Girard, *Violence and the Sacred* (Baltimore: Johns Hopkins University Press, 1977), p. 4.

POSTSCRIPT

1. Gaël De Santis, "En Italie, la chasse aux immigrés de Rosarno," *L'Humanité*, 11 January 2010.

INDEX

Note: Pages in italic type refer to illustrations.